Gold Rush on the Feather River

by G.C. Mansfield

with an introduction by Kerby Jackson

Introduction

It has been years since George C. Mansfield released his important publication "The Feather River in '49 and the Fifties". First released in 1924, this work has been unavailable to the mining community since those days, with the exception of expensive original collector's copies and poorly produced digital editions.

It has often been said that "*gold is where you find it*", but even beginning prospectors understand that their chances for finding something of value in the earth or in the streams of the Golden West are dramatically increased by going back to those places where gold and other minerals were once mined by our forerunners. Despite this, much of the contemporary information on local mining history that is currently available is mostly a result of mere local folklore and persistent rumors of major strikes, the details and facts of which, have long been distorted. Long gone are the old timers and with them, the days of first hand knowledge of the mines of the area and how they operated. Also long gone are most of their notes, their assay reports, their mine maps and personal scrapbooks, along with most of the surveys and reports that were performed for them by private and government geologists. Even published books such as this one are often retired to the local landfill or backyard burn pile by the descendents of those old timers and disappear at an alarming rate. Despite the fact that we live in the so-called "Information Age" where information is supposedly only the push of a button on a keyboard away, true insight into mining properties remains illusive and hard to come by, even to those of us who seek out this sort of information as if our lives depend upon it. Without this type of information readily available to the average independent miner, there is little hope that our metal mining industry will ever recover.

Though this volume may not at first seem to be of great importance to gold miners, I feel that those miners with an interest in smelting and refining their finds, especially those recovered from lodes, will find the processes outlined to be of great value.

This important volume and others like it, are being presented in their entirety again, in the hope that the average prospector will no longer stumble through the overgrown hills and the tailing strewn creeks without being well informed enough to have a chance to succeed at his ventures.

Please note that at times it is necessary to rearrange illustration plates in these texts. Any illustrations not found in their original sequence may be found following the index.

Kerby Jackson
Josephine County, Oregon
June 2015

www.goldminingbooks.com

The FEATHER RIVER in '49 and the Fifties

By GEORGE C. MANSFIELD, Author of "A History of Butte County" and "Butte: A California County"

Do you know where the real Californian is, the giant, the world builder? He is sitting by the trail, high up in the mountains. His eyes are dim and his head is white. His sleeves are lowered. His pick and shovel are by his side. His feet are weary and sore. He is still prospecting. Pretty soon he will sink his last prospect hole in the Sierras. Some younger man will come along and lengthen it out a little, and lay him in his grave. The old-timer will have passed out to prospect the outcroppings that star the floors of heaven.

And though he may die there in the pines on the mighty mountains, while still searching for the golden fleece, do not forget that his life is an epic, noble as any handed down from out the dusty old. Some day a fitting poet will come, and then he will take his place among the heroes and the gods.—Joaquin Miller.

The Days of Old, the Days of Gold
The Days of '49

Oh, it's here you see old Tom Moore, a relic of former days,
A bummer, too, they call me now, but what do I care for praise?
For my heart is filled with the days of yore, and oft do I repine,
For the days of old, the days of gold, the days of '49,
    For the days of old, the days of gold, the days of '49.

I had comrades, too, a saucy crew, hard cases I must confess;
But they were brave and true, my boys, as hunters from the West.
They would stand a pinch and never flinch, and never fret nor whine,
But like good old bricks, they stood the kicks in the days of '49,
    In the days of old, the days of gold, the days of '49.

There was Poker Bill, the fellow who was fond of playing tricks;
At a poker game he was always there and heavy, too, with bricks.
He'd ante a slug, or call for a draw or go you a handful blind,
But in the game of death he lost his breath, in the days of '49,
    In the days of old, the days of gold, the days of '49.

There was Monte Pete, I'll not forget the luck he always had,
He'd deal for you both night and day, as long as you had a scad.
One night a pistol laid him out; 'twas his layout in fine,
For it caught Pete sure and dead in the door in the days of '49,
    In the days of old, the days of gold, the days of '49.

There was New York Jake, the butcher boy, who was fond of getting tight,
And whenever he was on a spree was spoiling for a fight.
One day he ran against a knife in the hands of old Bob Kline,
And over Jake we held a wake, in the days of '49,
    In the days of old, the days of gold, the days of '49.

There was Buffalo Bill, who could out-roar a buffalo bull, you bet,
He roared all day and he roared all night, and I guess he's roaring yet.
One night he fell in a prospect hole; 'twas a roaring bad design,
For in that hole, he roared out his soul, in the days of '49,
    In the days of old, the days of gold, the days of '49.

There was old Lame Jess, a hated old case, who never would repent.
Jess never missed a single meal, and he never paid a cent.
But poor old Jess, like all the rest, to death did at last resign,
For in his bloom, he went up the flume, in the days of '49,
    In the days of old, the days of gold, the days of '49.

Now of all the comrades I had then, not one remains to boast;
They have left me here in my misery, like some poor wandering ghost;
And as I go from place to place, folks call me a traveling sign,
Saying, There's Tom Moore, a bummer sure, from the days of '49,
    From the days of old, the days of gold, the days of '49.
        —Popular ballad among the mining camps of California in the
                Middle Fifties.

The First "Strike" on the Feather

Toward the latter part of March, 1848, shortly after the discovery of gold by James Marshall at Coloma, on the American River, John Bidwell went to that place and saw for himself the scene of Marshall's epoch-making strike.

A keen observer and a careful student, Bidwell at once saw that physical conditions on the Feather River were much the same as on the American River where gold had been found. It is believed that Isaac Humphrey, who had some experience in gold mining in Georgia, was at Coloma at the time of Bidwell's visit and that he instructed Bidwell and others in methods of gold digging and gold washing

At any rate, Bidwell returned to his grant, now the site of Chico, called his neighbors together and told them of his belief that gold could be found in the gravel of the Feather River.

Following this meeting a prospecting party was formed and the work of prospecting for gold soon started. Soon the discovery of gold on the Feather River was heralded to the world. The date of Bidwell's strike at Bidwell Bar is generally given as July 4, 1848.

General Bidwell, in published recollections of his life, tells of this discovery as follows:

"On my return to Chico (from Coloma) I stopped over night at Hamilton, on the Feather River. On trying some of the sand in the river, I found light particles of gold, and reckoned that if light gold could be found that far down the river, the heavier particles would remain near the hills.

"On reaching Chico an expedition was organized, but it took sometime to get everything ready. We had to send twice up to Peter Lassen's mills to obtain flour; meat had to be dried; and we had to send to Sacramento after tools. Our party was Mr. Dickey, Potter, John Williams, William Northgraves and myself. We proceeded up the North Fork of the Feather River. In nearly all the places that we prospected we found colors. One evening while I camped at White Rock, Dicky and I in a short time panned out about an ounce of fine gold. The others refused to prospect any and said that the gold that we had obtained was so light that it wouldn't weigh anything. At this time we were all unfamiliar with the weight of gold dust, but I am satisfied what we had would weigh an ounce. Some of the men went to the American River to mine. Dickey Northgraves and I went to what is

JOHN BIDWELL
Who first discovered gold in the Feather River Diggings

now Bidwell Bar and there found gold and went to mining."

Warren T. Sexton, who came to California in 1849, and later became judge of the Superior Court of Butte County, has left some of the most valuable records of early days in the county. He gives some additional details of the first big strike of gold on the Feather. He writes in his reminiscences:

"Notice had been given to Bidwell's neighbors of his discovery at Hamil-

ton, and they each prepared themselves for the gold diggings with from fifty to one hundred Indians and their squaws, who were taken to the selected spot on the river and were supplied with beef driven from the several ranches from day to day, as necessity required.

"It would be only guesswork, or an average of the flying reports in circulation in 1849, to state the amount of gold dust taken home by these first miners. That it is very large there is no doubt. Some stories make it fabulous."

The discovery of gold on the Feather River served to increase the excitement in San Francisco over the momentous events that were transpiring but a few hundred miles from that city.

The first reports of Marshall's discovery had been received with skepticism there. Those who had first left San Francisco for the mines had done so rather secretively, through fear that if their mission were known it would subject them to ridicule. Continued reports, however, increased the interest, and by May, 1848, excitement was steadily growing.

Bancroft tells of the awakening of San Francisco in his history of California as follows:

"Among the comers to San Francisco was Samuel Brannan, the Mormon leader, who, holding up a bottle of dust in one hand and swinging his hat with the other, passed up the street shouting 'Gold! Gold!

Photo of a painting of Bidwell Bar as it was in the Gold Days. Across the river a train of pack mules will be observed coming down the trail to the town.

THE FIRST "STRIKE" ON THE FEATHER—*Continued*

Gold from the American River!' This took place early in May. The conversion of San Francisco was complete. Those who had hitherto denied a lurking faith, now unblushingly proclaimed it; and others who had refused to believe even in specimens exhibited before their eyes, hesitated no longer in accepting any reports, however exaggerated, and in speeding them onward duly magnified."

The reports of the Bidwell Bar strike increased the excitement of San Francisco. There were, however, some doubting Thomases.

The California Star had been the most skeptical of all the publications of that day concerning the importance and the veracity of the reports of gold strikes. Its comment on the report of Bidwell's discovery on the Feather River illustrates how exceedingly dangerous it is for a newspaper to attempt prophecy. Its report of this epochal event follows:

"There are rumors of a big excitement at Bidwell Bar and gold is said to be plentiful. The general idea here is that it is a scheme to dupe miners, as there is very little probability of gold being found in that vicinity."

Among the first to reach the Feather River diggings, other than those who left San Francisco, were Oregonians. The first emigrants reaching the Feather River in 1849, after the trip across the plains, attested the fact that they were instructed in the art of gold mining by Oregonians, who were already here. The mark of this early Oregon emigration still exists in the name Oregon City, a settlement of Butte County, and in the names of other places whose appellations were bestowed by Oregon miners.

Foreign countries heard of the new El Dorado even before the East learned of Marshall's discovery. These countries also sent their quota of gold miners to California. Instead of a handful of whites and some thousands of Indians, the Feather River area soon comprised as motley a population as could be found anywhere. Yankees, Southerners, English, Germans, French, Mexicans, Spaniards, Hawaiians, Peruvians, Chileans—all were to be found in the Feather River diggings, bound together by one common tie, the lust for gold.

Of the earlier emigration into the California gold mines, Bancroft has the following to say:

"Although the Americans maintained the ascendancy in numbers owing to readier access to the field, the stream of migration from foreign countries was great. Among the Asiatic nations the most deeply affected were the Chinese. With so much of the

Panning For Gold

gambling element in their dispositions, and so much of ambition, they turned over the tidings in their mind with feverish impatience, while their neighbors, the Japanese, heard of the gold discovery with startling indifference. Not less affected were the inhabitants of the Marquesas Islands. Those of the French colony who were

EAST HEARS FIRST NEWS OF FABULOUS FEATHER DIGGINGS

The East first heard of the Feather diggings through a letter written from California and published in the New York Journal of Commerce under date of August 29, 1849. The article reads: "At present the people are running over the country and picking gold out of the country here and there, just as hogs let loose in a forest would root out ground nuts. Some get eight or ten ounces of gold a day and the least active one or two. They make the most who employ wild Indians to hunt it for them. The wild Indians know nothing of its value and wonder what the palefaces want to do with it. The Indians will give an ounce of gold for the same weight of coined silver, or a thimbleful of glass beads. I know seven men who worked seven weeks and two days on the Feather River. They employed on an average fifty Indians, and got out of these seven weeks and two days, 275 pounds of pure gold."

These letters ran through the papers all over the country, creating wonder and amazement everywhere.

free made immediate departure, and were quickly followed by the military, leaving the governor alone to represent the government. On reaching Australia the news was eagerly circulated and embellished by shipmasters. The streets of the cities were placarded: 'Gold! Gold! Gold! In California!' Soon it became difficult to secure berths on departing vessels. So in Peru and Chile, where the California revelation was unfolded as early as September, 1848, by Colonel Mason's messenger on his way to Washington, the news brought a large influx in advance of the dominant United States immigration."

Much of this stream of travel was diverted to the Feather Diggings upon its arrival in California. It has left its mark in names of localities that still remain, although their origin is a matter of ignorance to many of the residents of the immediate vicinity. Thus we have Oregon City, survival of the great emigration of Oregonians; Kanaka Peak, marking a mining settlement of Hawaiian emigrants; Frenchtown, Spanishtown, Yankee Hill, and a number of like names.

Some further facts in the eventful career of John Bidwell may be of interest.

Born in New York, and moving west by successive stages, while a school teacher in Missouri, he assisted in organizing the Western Emigration Society, which conducted the first overland party into California. Many emigrants had made the journey to Oregon, but this was the first party organized to settle in California. At first five hundred people were associated in the Western Emigration Society, but the number diminished to sixty-nine. Knowing little of the route or the conditions before them, the party was fortunate in falling in with a band of missionaries led by the saintly Father De Smet, and guided by a trapper of wide experience, named Fitzpatrick. The missionaries were now on their way to the Flathead Indians, in what is now Idaho. They gave guidance and protection to the California party to the Great Salt Lake. About one-half of the Bidwell party, afraid to continue alone, remained with the De Smet band and finally made their way into Oregon.

Bidwell, with the remnant of his party, turned toward California. The party suffered thirst, hunger, cold, weariness, and the ever menacing danger of Indian attack. Finally the party was forced to abandon their wagons and push on with just such supplies as they could pack on their animals. A pass was at length found through the Sierras and the party reached California in 1841.

A $10,000 NUGGET—RECORD "CLEAN-UPS"

The Feather River District produced the famous "Dogtown Nugget," one of the world's largest gold chunks.

This nugget, found by mere chance in 1859, weighed fifty-four pounds and fifty pennyweights, fine gold. It netted $10,690. Its shape was something like that of a map of Africa. Its length was approximately the same as the diameter of a gold pan. The nugget was found on an hydraulic claim, which had one pipe in operation. On August 14th, 1859, while the proprietors of the claim were absent, one of the miners piped out the big nugget. The piece was in a slide from the side of the mountain. The principal owner of the mine, Ira Wetherbee, was in Dogtown, now known as Magalia, when the find was made.

In the afternoon several of the men employed by him came hurrying into Dogtown, picked him up from his chair, and set him on the counter. Wetherbee inquired in alarmed tones what had happened. They told him he would have to treat before he found out. This preliminary being concluded, the news was broken to him, and Magalia gave itself over to jollification for the remainder of the night.

In addition to the big nugget, the claim on that same day yielded $3000 more in gold The same week this claim yielded $30 000 in gold Two weeks' mining on the same claim resulted in finding seven nuggets, the smallest of which was worth over $2000.

The first pan of dirt taken out at Long's Bar is reported to have yielded $400 in gold.

In 1857 while working in the river above Oroville, John P. Leonard and H. B. Lathrop took out one pan containing one hundred and four ounces and four pennyweights of pure gold that sold for $2000.

Fluming companies netted as high as $30,672 in a day's operations.

The Cape Claim, two miles above Oroville, yielded one million dollars in sixty days' operations. From one pan $4000 in gold was obtained. It is related that one miner went down into one of the pump holes, and taking off his gum boots, filled them with gravel. When he panned the gravel it yielded $300 in gold.

The following records compiled from contemporary newspaper reports show the almost incredible richness of the Feather diggings:

In April, 1854, Charles Bader and Company took from their claim on the West Branch of the Feather River a lump of gold which brought $800.

In May, 1854, James Bader took out a nugget from his West Branch claim that weighed seven pounds.

In October, 1855, the treasurer of the High Rock Company came into Bidwell with forty-two pounds of gold dust and nuggets, the result of two days' labor.

In September, 1856, the Ohio Claim, a fluming operation, yielded $3000 in one day's run. The gold was so thick in the gravel, it could be seen with the naked eye.

In September 1856, the Junction Claim took out $18,000 in fourteen days' work. The receipts of the Rough and Ready Claim at the same time were given as running from $4000 to $5000 a day, with average expenses of $250 a day.

The Junction Claim the same year took out $564 in gold in one bucket and in ten hours' run took out $10,011.

EARLY POLITICS

The first county seat of Butte County was located at Hamilton, on the Feather River, just below Oroville, and named after a resident of the place, a nephew of Alexander Hamilton. Of this selection Judge Sexton writes as follows:

"The proprietors of Hamilton took an undue advantage of her sister towns by distributing deeds to a great many merchants and miners in the more populous precincts, of choice town lots, while to the more influential of the merchants, corner lots were deeded for business houses, all of which were accompanied by glowing descriptions of the future prosperity and wealth of the place. We do not accuse the honest miners of the time of being so sordid as to let this influence their votes, but Hamilton did receive a large majority over any other place."

The county seat of Butte County was shortly afterwards moved to Bidwell Bar and from Bidwell Bar to Oroville.

One of the interesting features of a trip over the Western Pacific is a great rock wall built in the center of the Feather River, and which passengers see immediately east of Oroville. This wall was built to divert the Feather River from its channel into another portion of the river bed in order that the gravel of the channel proper might be mined. The above view shows glimpses of this wall, which are even more plainly discernible from the passenger cars of the Western Pacific.

'49 Prices in the Feather River Gold Diggings

Prices in 1849 along the Feather River were as spectacular as was the mode of living and the occupation of the people there residing.

Flour and provisions sold at the uniform price of $1.25 a pound.

A drink of whisky was valued at a pinch of gold dust.

A barrel of whisky was no inconsiderable piece of property, for it usually brought the vendor thereof a good five thousand dollars.

As the mining population flocked in gold dust became more plentiful than the things it would buy, and prices soared to continually higher proportions.

Joseph Brown, who reached the Feather River in 1849, in a book of reminiscences of that year, states that a jar of pickles and two sweet potatoes cost him $11. He paid $7.50 for a paper of needles and two spools of thread.

Charles D. Ferguson, in a similar book, states that he paid $5 for two pears, and that he paid $2 for one onion.

"Up to this time," Ferguson writes, "there had been no fruit imported into the country, except dried apples and peaches, which were to be had at one dollar a pound. Dried Chili beans could be purchased at the same price. Pickled peaches cost $16 a gallon. So it is manifest that one had to make something to live; yet scarcely anyone stinted themselves. Board was $21 a week at the most common boarding houses. The food was mostly pork and beans and plenty of bread and beef, the latter being the cheapest article of food in the country. Such was the case wherever I went, up to the summer of 1851, when garden vegetables began to be raised plentifully."

With the development of the country and the establishment of stage and steamer routes and with the opening of roads, prices dropped to a more reasonable level. Market quotations of the middle Fifties show that the cost of living was not excessive.

Even, however, in the earlier period, the scale of prices appears to have met with but little objection on the part of the miners. The only trouble arose when some imposition was discovered The Butte Record reports an incident of this kind at Bidwell Bar, when a meeting of the miners was called "to take into consideration the action of a merchant who had been selling Dr. Strover's California Salve for butter."

Who the merchant was, or what happened, succeeding issues of the paper do not state.

Possibly the merchant advertised in its columns.

AN 1850 SERMON IN A LONG BAR GAMBLING HOUSE

Long Bar, now but a name and a memory, was in 1850 the most active mining camp upon the Feather River.

This camp furnished an incident that year typical of life in California in "the days of old." The story is told in one of the early histories of Butte County from which we quote:

"One bright summer morning in 1850, a gentleman rode into camp and began to inquire for a place where he could hold religious services. The only room that he could find was one devoted to gambling.

"As he entered the place, the play was running high. Ten thousand dollars in gold dust and nuggets was stacked upon the table. When the men were told of the preacher's wish, they stopped the game and listened to his sermon. At its close the hat was passed and $300 was deposited therein. Thanking the men, the preacher mounted his horse and rode away. At his departure the game was continued with renewed interest."

Judge C. F. Lott, a pioneer of '49, has told the story of the first sermon preached in Butte County. One Sunday morning a preacher came to Adamstown, a camp located just across the Feather River from Long's Bar. He talked with George Adams, who was a pious man for those days. Adams arranged for a service on Sunday morning. This service was attended by nearly one thousand miners.

The minister preached an able and interesting sermon, and when the collection was taken he received a hatful of gold dust and nuggets. That night he crossed the river, and went to Long's Bar. He entered the Blue Tent, a famous gambling resort, and becoming interested in one of the games, began betting. He was not as successful at gambling, however, as he had been at preaching. Before morning he did not have enough of his morning collection left to pay for his breakfast. So the miners, who had been pleased with his sermon, passed the hat, and presented him with $304 in gold, just as he was leaving the camp.

One of the best known of the itinerant preachers of the period was "Father" Taylor, a Methodist street preacher, who made his way into California in 1849.

"Father" Taylor relates in his reminiscences that he preached one Sunday morning at Long's Bar to a large audience. He was encouraged by what he saw to expect a much larger one in the afternoon, but when afternoon came he found a congregation of only twenty persons, as everybody else had become drunk.

In his denunciation of Sabbath breakers, "Father" Taylor called attention to the blacksmith at Long's Bar, whom he described as "an excellent man, well spoken of by everybody, the best man in the mountains," but who confessed to "working at his forge on Sunday for the accommodation of miners who came to town only on that day."

"Shades of the Fathers!" exclaimed Taylor. "If this is the best man in the mountains, the Lord pity the worst!"

Another famous evangelist of the mining camps was Parson McGrath. McGrath covered a territory extending from Western Nevada down through the Feather Diggings and including all intermediate territory.

Through this territory he held revivals and pleaded with the irreligious to forsake the ways of the diggings and to leave the paths of sin for those of righteousness. At last at one of these revivals held in Honey Lake Valley, Pastor McGrath won to righteousness one of the toughest characters of the place, one who was so conscious of his sin that he believed immersion only could wash it away.

John L. Considine tells the story as follows:

"It was late in the fall, and the water was ice cold. Parson and convert were in the lake, bodies shivering, teeth chattering, and the gooseflesh standing out all over them like buttons on a fat man's vest. A profound hush hovered over the assembled congregation. The parson read the service and dipped the convert. As he raised him above the water again, the neophyte sputtered:

" 'Oh,———— that water's cold!'

"Convinced by this burst of profanity that traces of sin remained, the parson promptly dipped the sinner a second time. As the convert's dripping face emerged once more, he uttered another ejaculation:

" 'That's————cold water!'

"McGrath instantly plunged him under for another laving, and when he came up for the third time he maintained a discreet silence."

The parson's congregation in one place was so small and poor that he was forced to eke out his ministerial stipend by manual labor. He took up the painter's trade, but suffered from painter's colic. Learning that whisky afforded relief, he tried it. It was near the end of the week and he absorbed enough of the remedy to acquire what was known as "a hang-over." On Sunday morning he ascended the pulpit with a not altogether steady step and delivered an address so extremely unorthodox that he had a hard time later on to win back the congregation, although he explained that his erratic conduct was due to the effects of "colic cure."

He afterwards became chaplain of the Nevada legislature, and was much annoyed by the protests of a legislator, who insisted that the invocation was a nuisance.

"If the parson would pray for something useful, I wouldn't mind," said the lawmaker, who happened also to be a miner. The next morning McGrath opened the day's session with a prayer substantially like this:

"Oh, Lord, we pray thee to remember Assemblyman Robinson! May the rock in his tunnel become as soft as his head and the water in his ditch as abundant as the whisky he daily drinks. Amen."

And Assemblyman Robinson complained no more.

The records tell similar stories of other ministers of pioneer days.

Stages Race Across the Sierras

Old picture of stage coach on the California and Oregon Stage Line

In 1857 Congress made a large appropriation to construct a wagon road across the plains and into California. Immediately the question of the location of the California end of the transcontinental highway became a subject of heated controversy. Oroville and Marysville in particular, were strenuous advocates of differing routes, which they believed would be of particular advantage to them. Finally, as the controversy grew more bitter, rival expeditions were fitted out, and the first stage coach race across the Sierra Nevada Mountains was projected.

The Oroville expedition left on May 20, 1857. The stage was adorned with banners bearing the following legend: "Pioneer stage coach across the Nevada Mountains—Oroville to Honey Lake—U. S. Mail route."

Whatever fear as to the route was dispelled by the progress that the stage coach made. Honey Lake, where the transcontinental highway was to enter California, was reached in forty-three hours' driving time. The party was given a royal reception there. It was some time later that the Marysville representatives arrived, and they were forced to admit many hardships.

The register of the Roop House, a famous hostelry in the Honey Lake Valley in the early days, tells the story of the arrival of the Oroville delegation, as follows:

"June 3, 1857. Orevill dilegation in with first coach ever in the valley. W. A. Gamble, Alex Brown, S. McDermott, H. B. Hunt, Thos. Galloway. Charles J. Brown report the road from Orevill to Honey Lake Valley excellent.

"June 7. Orevill coach leaves at 10 o'clock p. m., all O. K. A salute."

THE FIRST INDICTMENT

The first indictment in Butte County was returned in June, 1851. It was brought against the slayers of Cassius Paris, a Mexican. The evidence showed that Paris had threatened to kill four of his countrymen, and that they had captured him with lariats and shot him to death. The jury declared that Paris had received just what he deserved, and turned the men loose.

The rivers were crossed in the early days by means of ferries. These ferries were generally about sixty feet by twelve feet, inside measurement. They were propelled by the current of the river.

The recovery of gold from the California placers is over $1,416,671,616.

Sutter Fort at Sacramento

BIRTH OF OROVILLE, ONE OF CALIFORNIA'S FIRST "GOLD TOWNS"

As elsewhere in the gold diggings, so in the Feather River District, "cities" sprang up almost over night.

A newspaper of September, 1855, gives an account of the birth, or rather the re-birth of Oroville and at the same time portrays a characteristic picture of California towns in the early gold period. It says:

"Mining towns, like mushrooms, spring up in a night. A party of prospecting miners strike a good lead and pitch their tents; others crowd in a board shanty is put up and some enterprising person starts a store with a hundred dollars' worth of shovels, picks, flannel shirts and tools; soon an express is started to the nearest large town—and they are in full blast.

"Six weeks ago the present town of Oroville was started. The town is in Butte County, on the right bank of the Feather River, about 27 miles by stage from Marysville, and opposite Table Mountain. The site is a level, sandy bottom. The hills on the other side of the ravine rise some 200 feet and are supposed to contain plenty of yellow dust."

Things moved rapidly in Oroville, as we find the same paper recording in July, 1856, the following facts relative to Oroville's growth:

"It is astonishing the rapidity with which buildings are being erected in Oroville. Yesterday we noticed the corner stones (four herring boxes) of a building were being placed in position to receive the lumber of the surface. In the evening the building was occupied and taking in boarders."

The statement is probably not exaggerated, as the buildings of the early period consisted chiefly of sticks poles or anything upon which canvas could be stretched.

A contemporaneous view of Oroville in the middle Fifties is given by the Butte Record in its issue of December 6, 1856. Under the heading "Our Village," the editor of that paper wrote as follows:

"Business seems to be in a flourishing condition. Loafers are plenty without cash, and whisky is plenty for cash. Jumping lots and suing and being sued, occupy the attention of some folks. Fighting and horse racing are favorite amusements. Loafers seem busy loafing and men of business appear busy in their several vocations. Women and children are tolerably plenty; and mud, mules and miners greatly abound. Stages come and go crowded, and boarding houses and beds are crowded all the time. Sports and doctors continue to deal out cards and physic. Great gangs of

The above picture is a photograph of a drawing made of Oroville about eighteen months after the city's birth. The drawing was made from the north bank of the Feather River, and the original bears the following inscription: "The town of Oroville and the County Seat of Butte County, of which the above is an accurate view, is situated on the south bank of the Feather River where the stream enters the Sacramento Valley. It is one of those places which only California enterprise could produce, its age is less than eighteen months, yet in population, of commercial importance, it is the fourth town in the State. Every kind of mining is conducted here, with unexampled success—surface, deep, tunnel, hydraulic and river diggings. The population of Oroville and adjacent mining territory is about 4500."

worthless dogs disturb the rest of quiet citizens who want to sleep. All sorts of things are continually occurring in private circles that ought not to be published, and few things happen that ought to be put into the papers."

The Butte Record in December, 1856, tells the story of the first settlement of Oroville as follows: "The emigrants of '49—those who came by the Lawson Horn and many of those who sought the northern mines, centered on the spot where Oroville now

stands and a city of tents dignified by the name Ophir, sprang into existence. Here are yet visible the little mounds of earth that tell a melancholy tale of the severities of the overland journey and of the winter of '49 and '50. The rich surface diggings of other sections scattered the denizens of Ophir to other sections, and a solitary tenement remained, which in its loneliness has often endured the scrutiny of wondering deer and antelopes and the nocturnal inspection of the grizzly."

A street view in Oroville's Chinatown section which at one time housed 10 000 Chinese, and was second only to San Francisco in its Chinese population. This is one of the few typical "Chinatowns" that remain in California.

The Famous Gold Lake Stampede

One of the most colorful adventures of California's gold days has its setting in the Feather River Canyon.

Stoddard, an emigrant of 1849, became lost in the mountains, with a companion, and the two attempted to find their way out.

According to the story told by Stoddard, who was the only one to reach white settlements, he and his companion stopped to drink at a lake and saw among the moss at the edge of the lake chunks of pure gold.

In their anxiety to find their way out of the mountains, imperfect observations of the place were taken. The next day Stoddard and his companion were attacked by Indians. Stoddard was struck in the heel by an arrow, but escaped. His companion was never heard from again. Stoddard finally reached the mining settlements where he told his story.

The winter was setting in, and it was impossible at that time to attempt to reach his "gold lake." The story was carried from mining camp to mining camp. To those who declared that Stoddard was crazy, the answer was made that he had the gold specimens to substantiate his story.

In May, 1850, a party of twenty-five miners was organized by Stoddard to go to his lake. This party was followed by fully 500 other miners, who clung to the heels of the party of twenty-five, watching their every movement.

When the locality where the lake was supposed to be situated was reached, Stoddard was unable to locate the lake and wandered about from place to place in an aimless fashion.

The miners then called a meeting. Some declared that Stoddard was crazy; others thought that he had heard of the lake and ascribed its discovery to himself; others still believed in Stoddard's story, but thought he had become confused as to its location.

It was finally decided to hang Stoddard. He was, however, given a respite of twenty-four hours and told to find the lake in that time or die. Stoddard, however, managed to slip quietly out of camp that night and escaped. The next morning the miners disbanded.

Reaching the mines, Stoddard attempted to organize another company to search for the lake, but no one would attach any credence to his story, and Stoddard disappeared from the pages of California history.

There are a number of different versions and explanations of the affair, ranging from the theory that Stoddard was crazy, to declarations that his story was true, that the lake existed, but that it had been filled in by a landslide.

Gold Lake, a few miles from Blairsden, for some unknown reason, is supposed to be the lake for which Stoddard was searching. Humbug Valley, but a little way from Belden, gets its name from the fact that the search ended there and Stoddard's humbuggery was there discovered.

One result of the Gold Lake rush, however, was the discovery of some rich diggings in Plumas County, and another extension of the early mining area.

Gold Lake, near Blairsden, which legend fixes as the objective of the "Gold Lake Stampede," the most famous of California's gold rushes.

FEATHER'S GOLDEN GRAVELS MINED BY WINGDAMS AND FLUMES

The Feather River and its "Forks" were the scene in the early days of extensive mining by the wing-dam method.

The wing-dam was an enclosure of the river, made by a head-dam and a foot-dam, and connected by a wall. These dams were made either of rock walls, filled with dirt, or more usually from plank cribbing, filled with rock and dirt.

The function of the head-dam was to turn the river, and that of the foot-dam to keep out the back-water.

The gravel was usually drained by means of Chinese pumps. These were wheels with buckets attached, which were sometimes operated by the flowing stream, but more generally by man power.

In this manner the water in the river would be turned, the bed of the river drained, and the gold recovered from the gravel.

Another method of river mining consisted of the turning the river by blasting a new channel to carry it.

"The flumes," says an account of mining operations along the Feather River, published in a newspaper in July, 1854, "are interspersed with wing-dams, bank diggings and Chinese camps."

INDIAN LEGEND TOLD OF GOLD LAKE ON THE MIDDLE FEATHER

When the news of Marshall's discovery of gold at Coloma became public, and the Indians became informed of the eagerness of the white man to acquire it, they confided the "Gold Lake Legend" to Captain Sutter.

Their story went far back in the Sierras, snuggled down between high cliffs of quartz containing fabulous quantities of gold, there was a gold lake inhabited by an aquatic monster. The Indians were afraid to venture near the place, for this slimy, green dragon would catch Indians, good or bad, and swallow them whole. So no Indian sought the vicinity of the gold lake, nor would they attempt to show any white man where it was.

From the description given, the legendary lake seems to apply to the Nelson ledge, near Butte Bar, in Plumas County, where it had been cut through by the Middle Fork of the Feather River, thereby exposing an immense quartz vein over five feet through from which rich specimens were taken in the early days.

Little drops of water,
Little grains of gold,
Make our bellies full of
All the grub they'll hold.
—From a Parody of the Fifties.

Rich Bar, Where Burros Packed Out Nuggets

* * * * * * * * * * * * * * * *

Battle Over a Gold Claim That Losers Won

Rich Bar!

In "the days of gold" a thriving, hustling mining camp of twenty-five hundred people, and in the early Fifties the largest town in the northern diggings! A place where only burros could be used to bring supplies down the mountain side and where the burros went back up the mountain fairly groaning under the load of gold they carried.

Rich Bar! Yesterday a place where millions of dollars in gold was taken from its gravels, where fortunes were made and fortunes lost! Today a pine-covered mountainside, a few uncared-for apple trees, a whistling station for the Western Pacific, with only the scars left by the miners and the monument that the Native Sons of the Golden West have erected to bear witness to its former glory.

Rich Bar was among the early places where gold was struck on the Feather River. It was probably found by one of the disappointed gold seekers who had gone on the Gold Lake quest. According to the story that has been handed down almost as a legend, three Germans came down the river on a prospecting trip and camped for the night at the head of the bar. It was while going for their water that one of them passed over the high, barren bedrock at the mouth of French Creek and saw that the cracks and crevices in the rocks were literally filled with flakes of the precious metal. The Germans staked out three claims, so the story goes, and in the next four days took out $36,000 in nuggets and gold dust.

News of the bonanza strike soon reached the miners who were mining on Nelson Creek, Poorman's Creek and the other streams nearby, and the big rush was on. The gravel of Rich Bar was found to be fabulously rich in virgin gold. It is reported that one miner took out $2900 in two pans of gravel and that this incident led to calling the place "Rich Bar."

It was the richest strike that had yet been made either in the Feather diggings or, in fact, in California. Despite the difficulties of communication that then existed, the news of the discovery traveled as if by magic and in a few days the bar was lined with eager gold seekers. Within a few weeks the mining area extended four miles down the river.

So rich was the gravel that claims on the bar itself were limited to ten feet square, while those farther down the river and on the hillsides were forty feet square.

The amount of gold taken out during

The above picture is that of the Rich Bar monument. The inscription reads: "Erected by the Native Sons of the Golden West to the memory of the pioneers who settled on this spot, some of whom found rest on the hillside near this monument; and as typifying pioneer motherhood of California, this monument is particularly dedicated to Nancy Ann Bailey, who died in the performance of her duty to God, Country, and Race, June 1, 1850."

the first summer and the summer following is fabulous. It has been variously estimated at from three to four millions of dollars. Some claims paid better than others. If a miner happened to have a deep and wide crevice running through his claim, his "clean-up" would run into huge sums. Single pans of dirt frequently yielded from $1500 to $2000. One company of four

men took out over $50,000 in a few hours' time.

Enoch Judson related that he had a claim on Smith Hill. He carried the dirt to the river in a flour sack, and frequently washed as high as $750 in gold from one sack of dirt.

During the first few weeks the only implements the miners had were picks, shovels and gold pans. But with the first rush for claims over, they built rockers and with these would handle ten times the dirt that they had been able to handle with the picks, shovels and pans.

It was at Rich Bar that one of the most exciting battles of the early Fifties took place, a battle that was recounted in mining camps for years, and a battle that the winners lost and the losers won.

A band of Americans and a band of Frenchmen arrived at the Bar almost at the same time. Their operations resulted in a conflict of interest almost from the first. Instead of the two bands settling their differences by battle, however, it was decided that each band would pick one of their number and that the two would fight together; that the band whose champion lost, would move from the ground, leaving it to the victors.

The Americans selected their man and the Frenchmen named their representative. The two were powerful, quick, agile, heavily muscled and as hard as nails.

The place for the fight was named. There were neither rules nor gloves.

The men approached each other warily and then the battle began. Encouraged by the cheers of their backers, and the prize of rich gold diggings they fought like tigers. Bleeding and bruised they fought on and on. Finally victory came to the American, when his adversary lay senseless on the ground, unable to rise.

The Frenchmen, true to their bargain, left the ground in dispute. They moved farther up on the Bar to new claims, and uncovered the richest diggings of rich Rich Bar. Thus victory came to the losers. The place is remembered today by the old name, French Gulch.

Nancy Ann Bailey, who came there with her husband, Peter Bailey, a member of a Virginia company, was the first woman to brave the perils of the trip into the rough and rocky mountain canyon. And she was the first person to die there. It is to Nancy Ann Bailey, who died there in

(Continued on Page 27)

When Courts Made Their Own Precedents

The early records of Butte County are filled with amusing incidents of the free and easy manner in which the early courts acted in administering justice.

An interesting incident illustrative of early judicial methods is related under date of February 4, 1856, in the Butte Record. Ferries across the Feather River formed a never failing subject of litigation. This litigation came under the jurisdiction of the Court of Sessions, over which Judge Moses Bean presided.

One case, involving a ferry near Oroville, was appealed from Judge Bean's court, and the district court reversed the ruling made by His Honor.

At the next term of the Court of Sessions, another ferry case involving precisely the same issues arose, and was decided by Judge Bean exactly as he had decided the first case.

We will let the Record tell the rest of the story:

"Peaceable, quiet and patient as lawyers are known to be when cases are decided against them, this was entirely too much for counsel. Springing to his feet he began to protest. The Court, with the dignity and gravity so becoming the Bench, interrupted the counsel.

"'Sit down, sir, and keep quiet,' ordered the Court. 'This Court would advise you to keep your shirt on. The Court does not wish to be interrupted in giving its decisions. The Court is aware that the District Court overruled the decision of this court in a case where the same issues arose, but that does not matter.'

"Here the Judge paused a moment, passed his fingers through his hair, stuck both thumbs in the armholes of his vest, laid both feet on the top of his desk and, with an unusual look of dignity, continued: 'If the Superior Cour 5 of this State have a mind to make damn fools of themselves, that is no reason why this Court should. Mr. Clerk, enter up the decision. Court adjourned.'"

The North Californian, also published in Oroville, in its issue of December, 1855, reports a scene in the Recorder's Court in Oroville. An attorney in pleading, addressed the Court as follows:

"If the Court please. I believe that the witness is by his own showing interested in the outcome of this case. I object on that ground to his further testimony. If a man may swear himself into the possession of $200 worth of property, all I have to say is that this is a hell-roaring pretty court of justice."

To which the Court is reported to have replied:

TRIBUTE TO THE PIONEERS

Hittell, in his history of California, pays the following tribute to the character of the pioneers:

"The pioneers were the most active, industrious and enterprising body of men, in proportion to their numbers, that was ever thrown together to form a new community. Four-fifths of them were young men, between eighteen and thirty-five years of age. They came from all sections of the country and many of them from foreign countries. They all came to labor or found, when they got to the mines, that to keep on an equality with their neighbors, they had to labor. Next to the tendency in the mining regions to remove all restraints, and to bring into prominence all the vices that were lurking, perhaps unknown to themselves, in the breasts of many of the first comers, one of the most noticeable features of the mines was the extraordinary leveling tendency of that life— a tendency, upon the effects of which have been based to a great extent, the re-adjustments and developments on new lines that have constituted the peculiarities of Californian civilization. Every man finding every other man compelled to labor, found himself the equal of every other man; and as the labor required was physical, rather than mental, the usual superiority of head-workers over hand-workers disappeared entirely. This condition of things lasted several years. Men who had been governors and legislators and judges in the old States, worked by the side of outlaws and convicts; scholars and students by the side of men who could not read or write. Old social distinctions were obliterated; everybody did business on his own account, and not one man in ten was the employee, and much less the servant, of another."

"This Court permits no profane language in its presence. Your language seems too damned profane. You are fined $5 for contempt of Court." The attorney thereupon called His Honor's attention to the fact that the language of the court was also rather strong, and suggested that in view of that fact the fine should be remitted. But instead of remitting the attorney's fine, the court fined itself $5 for contempt of itself, paid the fine and insisted that the attorney do likewise.

"Squire" Wright of Chico also figured largely in early court proceedings. The records tell of one case in which General John Bidwell, later a candidate of the Prohibition party for the presidency, was a party. Both General Bidwell and his opponent had race horses, of which they were very proud.

After hearing the evidence "Squire" Wright suggested that the issues involved be decided by a race between the two horses. Plaintiff and defendant agreed, and the court, the parties to the action and the spectators adjourned to a track where the race was held. General Bidwell's horse won the race, and "Squire" Wright entered a decision in the case in his favor.

It was this same "Squire" Wright who sentenced a culprit to be hung for a very minor offense of which he had been found guilty. When the lad's attorney objected, declaring that the "Squire" would be overruled, the reply was that there was no overruling of that Court. It was only with extreme difficulty that the "Squire" was finally convinced that a jail sentence was the extreme penalty that could be meted out in the case.

Another of the early institutions of the Feather River diggings was "Squire" Bonner, peregrinating justice of Plumas County.

Realizing that but little business would come to him at Holme's Hole, on Rush Creek, where he resided, "Squire" Bonner put his "justice shop" on wheels. The story is told in an early history of Plumas County. He traveled from camp to camp in search of controversies that he could adjudicate and fees that he could collect. A single volume having the appearance of a law book was his badge of authority and his book of reference for all classes of cases that came before him.

Thus equipped, so the story goes, he made his appearance at Nelson Point one day and soon a case was before him for adjudication. The testimony soon developed that the plaintiff was "broke" and that there was little hope of fees from him.

It was the rule of "Squire" Bonner to decide against the party who was best able to pay the costs. The plaintiff had nothing, so Bonner planned to decide in his favor and thus throw costs on the defendant. The evidence was such, however, that he feared that he would not be able to collect his fees. He therefore made an order that the defendant be required to give bonds for the cost of the suit and for $500 damages, so

(Continued on Page 28)

HOW SLAVES WERE MADE FREE BY GOLD DIGGERS OF FEATHER

The thought of slavery is generally not associated with early life in California, or with the men who came here in '49 and the Fifties to mine for gold.

And yet, the first document recorded in the official records of Butte County is a deed of manumission, given by Franklin Stewart to his slave, Washington. This grant of freedom was under date of May 4, 1852, and reads as follows:

"Free papers of the slave, Washington, from Franklin Stewart.

"State of California, County of Butte.

"Know all men by these presents, that I, Franklin Stewart, of the County and State aforesaid, for and in consideration of seventeen years faithful servitude of my slave, Washington, rendered by him in the States of Arkansas and Missouri, do hereby set free and emancipate him, the said slave—his age about 34 years; color, slight copper—and fully relinquish all right unto the said slave Washington, which I might be entitled to in law or in equity.

"Given under my hand and seal this 4th day of May, 1852.
"FRANKLIN STEWART."

There are other records of similar documents, and in fact, the manumission of slaves was quite common in California during the early days.

A decision of the Supreme Court made it illegal to hold a slave here when brought here for profit or residence; but many slaves generally from a feeling of attachment to their masters, refused to avail themselves of the opportunity afforded under the decision to gain their freedom, some even returning to the East with their masters.

The following affidavit, made at White Rock, on the Feather River, in 1853, is of interest in this connection:

Some time in the Spring or Summer of the year A. D. 1851, there came to Ophir, Butte County, California, a man calling himself Samuels, who said that he had control of a colored man called Lewis Taylor, and that the said Taylor was to work for the said Samuels (or some relative, I am not certain which) for one year. But after the said Taylor, working about six months, he made an agreement with the said Samuels that he would be a free man if the said Taylor would pay unto the said Samuels the sum of $500 in good, clean gold dust, which the said Taylor requested me to pay to the said Samuels, when I advised him not to do so, because the said Samuels could not show any right to receive it. But the said

An April Fool Election

It is an interesting commentary on the Feather River section that its political history begins with an April Fool election.

The State Legislature on March 2, 1850, passed an act providing that elections should be held in the newly designated counties of the State for the selection of county officers and the organization of county government.

There lived at Long's Bar a character widely known as "Old Dick" Stuart—intelligent, sharp witty, and withal a most inveterate joker, with a decided preference for "practical" jokes.

Without waiting for the official notice to come calling the election, Stuart called it himself in Butte County, fixing the first Monday of April as the date. He persuaded the voters of the county of the correctness of the action, the uncertainty of the mail service furnishing a reason why they should proceed without formal notice from the State government.

Candidates for county offices announced themselves and started campaigning for votes. Several red hot contests developed.

The Suspension Bridge at Bidwell Bar is one of the structures built by the pioneers that still remain intact. The cables were brought around the Horn, and the bridge built in 1854.

Taylor insisted that I should pay him, which I did.

A. G. SIMPSON.

Subscribed and sworn to before me at my office at White Rock, this, the 19th day of April, A. D. 1853.

J. R. HOPE, J. P.

The polls opened sharp on time, and all day long the candidates and their friends labored with voters.

Busiest of all was "Old Dick" Stuart, who, with voice, money and liquor electioneered all day long.

The polls closed and the vote was counted. Just as the successful candidates were beginning to celebrate their victory, Stuart called their attention to the day, to the fact that the election was unauthorized, and to the further fact that the first Monday in April and April 1st in that year fell on the same day. The announcement served only to increase the hilarity of the celebration. The night of April 1st, 1850, is declared to have been one of the "largest" nights in both the early and later history of Butte County.

As for "Old Dick" Stuart, he declared the election the most successful April Fool's joke he had ever played.

The records of Butte County are entirely devoid of either a tabulation of the vote cast at its first election or reference to this election. Were it not for the memoirs of the pioneers, the county's first election would be a matter of forgotten history.

Mere technicalities were considered as unnecessary encumbrances when the real election was held for the organization of the county. This election was held on June 10, 1850. The Board of Inspectors in certifying to the election returns accompanied them with a resolution in which they "resolved" that "a too strict regard for mere technicalities in the law would have the effect of defeating, rather than furthering, the ends of justice," and accordingly these technicalities were overlooked by election officials.

In an official protest filed, some of the technicalities "overlooked" were enumerated as follows:

At Hamilton, the number of votes cast exceeded the number of inhabitants of the place.

At Bidwell Bar, the formality of swearing in the election officers was "overlooked."

At American Bar, there was but one inspector and no judges, that inspector being himself a candidate for office.

The court refused to pay any attention to the protest, and the canvass of the board stood.

An epitaph on a '49 tombstone in a pioneer graveyard of the Feather District:

"A renegade cuss, here he lies;
Nobody laughs, nobody cries;
Where he's gone, how he fares;
Nobody knows, nobody cares."

Fluming the Feather for Its Gold

The Feather River was the scene of the largest fluming operations in California. These operations extended from Oroville to the junction of the North Fork and Middle Fork, seven miles east of Oroville.

In these fluming operations the Feather River was literally lifted from its bed and carried in flumes for miles in order that the golden treasure that its gravels carried, might be wrested from the stream bed.

Flume mining along the Feather was at its height in 1856 and 1857. Contemporaneous newspaper accounts state that "the success of the river claims this year (1856) is unparalleled in the history of gold mining. Not one claim on the river, whether it be flume, coffer-dam or wing-dam, but reports good success. The countenances of our miners are most pleasing to behold. They are as full of laugh as their blasted skins can hold."

At Randolph Point, on the South Fork of the Feather River, a portion of the river bed, not over 1000 feet in length, yielded over $2,000,000 in

View showing a flume on the Feather River above Oroville

gold in fluming operations. This was in the Middle Fifties. Twenty years later a band of Chinamen worked the same gravel. One spot of virgin gravel was found that the early miners had not discovered. From one bucket of gravel the Chinamen obtained over $10,000.

QUARTZ MINING WITH MULES

The year 1850 saw the beginning of quartz mining along the Feather River. During the years 1850 to 1852, quartz mining was active all over the State, and many locations were made in Butte County. It was during this period that the first quartz mining was done in Forbestown. In 1852 Sir Henry Huntley, who represented British mining capital, built a stone arrastra in Forbestown. After crushing quite a few tons of ore, he placed the pulp into a hollow vat, added water and

some chemicals. This done, he had a couple of mules tramp around through this pulp in a circle—an ancient method in Spanish America for the treatment of silver ore minus the chemicals. The chemicals evidently had more effect on the mules than the ore, for their hoofs fell off. This incident put both the mining company and the mules out of business.

After 1852 the quartz excitement abated, and the attention of Butte miners was centered on placer mining. In 1854 there were thirteen quartz mining companies in Butte County. Some of these claims proved rich in gold.

LACK OF CHILDREN, EDUCATION OBSTACLE

Just as courts of law and organized government followed immediately after the arrival of the miners, so also schools were soon established. In 1851 it was reported that there were not then in Butte County more than fifty school children. It must be remembered that Butte County then included the area now in Plumas County and portions of Lassen and Colusa Counties. In 1852 the county assessor reported that there were not enough children in the county to form a school, and for that reason no districts had been formed. The next year, however, saw the organization of three schools.

One of these first schools is described by A. E. Swain, a teacher of the early period, as follows: "The school was held in a cabin, about ten by twelve feet square, three sides of which were of logs, while the other was made of sluice boxes piled one on top of the other. The cabin was without windows unless you chose to so call a couple of holes, eighteen inches square, cut in the sides. It had a dirt floor, had but one door and had not the least article of school furniture or apparatus. An old greasy table in the middle of the room for the teacher, and a few benches for the scholars, constituted the furniture. The school numbering some ten or twelve pupils, was taught by a tall, lank, one-eyed man, whose only redeeming feature was his ability to chastise the erring juveniles."

View of mining operations being carried on in the bed of the Feather River in the days when the stream itself was carried in great flumes to permit mining the gravel of its channel. Nowhere in the State was fluming carried on as extensively as it was along the Feather River above Oroville. There were dozens of these fluming companies operating in the Middle Fifties and an enormous quantity of gold was taken out by them.

Outwitting Judge Lynch

Lynch law was administered by the miners of the gold period in California's history first as a matter of necessity, due to the absence of court and officers, and later because of the emigration into the mines of hard and desperate characters.

However, Judge Lynch was not always successful in his operations.

An instance of the failure of lynch law occurred in Natchez, a thriving mining camp of the Feather diggings in the Fifties, and now an almost forgotten spot.

A number of highway robberies had been committed near Natchez, and both officers and a posse of citizens were searching for the perpetrators of the crimes.

W. W. Hobart, while some seven miles away from Natchez, heard that one of the robbers had been captured and taken to Natchez, where he was to be lynched.

Mounting his horse, the officer made quick time to Natchez. He found the accused man tied to a horse post, with his back against the post. Nearby, within a few feet, a fine horse, saddled and bridled, was tied.

Hobart tied his own horse near by. Some of the mob informed Hobart that as an officer he had no business there; that they knew the prisoner was guilty; that they were going to hang him; and that if Hobart interfered, he would have a fight on his hands.

Hobart laughed at the men, assured them that he did not intend to interfere, and strolled among the crowd, laughing and joking and talking as the others did to the prisoner. Watching his opportunity, he whispered to the man:

"Can you ride for your life?"

"Yes," was the reply.

"I will cut these ropes on your wrist," Hobart told him, "but you must stand still and do not move your hand till I tell you, and then up the hill!"

The excited crowd took but little notice of what Hobart was doing, as a trial was being arranged in order that the lynching might have at least some appearance of law.

Hobart took advantage of this situation. He deftly untied the horse near the prisoner, leaving the halter on the hitching post.

After chatting casually with some of the men, he remarked, "Well, I don't see that I can do this fellow any good, so that I might as well be going." The men assented to this, glad to get rid of an officer.

Hobart untied his own horse, jockeying his position so that he and the animal were between the crowd and the prisoner and with the prisoner next to the unmounted horse.

"Now!" he said to the prisoner.

In an instant the man was on the horse, and away officer and prisoner went at breakneck speed.

So great was the surprise of the crowd that the men were out of pistol

range before the firing commenced. Before rifles could be brought to bear, they were out of sight.

Hobart brought his man to Oroville, and put him in the county jail. Later he was regularly tried, convicted and sent to the State prison.

Until the last half of the Fifties, attention to agriculture was so scanty in Butte County that it can be considered as nil. As mining required more capital and gold became less abundant, attention turned to agriculture and horticulture.

BETTING A GOLD CLAIM ON THE ELECTION OF PRESIDENT BUCHANAN

Partisanship ran high in the Fifties among the miners along the banks of the Feather River.

The miners took their politics seriously. Their party was one that could do no wrong, while the other party could do nothing right.

An advertisement that appeared in the Butte Record of October 11, 1856, indicates the intensity of party feeling during the decade. The advertisement follows:

"I, the undersigned, James M. Major, being willing to risk pretty nearly everything short of my eternal existence, upon the election of James Buchanan to the presidency, hereby offer for sale, six claims situated about 1000 yards from the Courthouse in Oroville, all furnished with sluices, cabin, tools, etc., that will pay from $3 to $5 per day to the man, and perhaps more, one-half to be paid down and the other half when James Buchanan shall be elected President of the United States. Miners are invited to examine the claims and satisfy themselves of their value

"JAMES M. MAJOR.

"Oroville, October 4, 1856."

JUSTICE MOVED SPEEDILY WHEN THE MINERS HELD COURT

The miners had a rapid and satisfactory manner of punishing offenses against the law. No appeals were permitted and penalty followed immediately upon the pronouncement of sentence. The Miners' Court was an institution venerated and respected by the law abiding citizens and feared by all evil doers.

Ordinary disputes between miners over claims and like matters were settled easily, but if felonies were committed the procedure was more elaborate.

When a case arose, the miners were called to assemble, usually in the largest saloon. The business began by the election of a chairman, or a judge, depending upon the nature of the business coming before the assembly. If a criminal case, a sheriff, a jury, a counsel for the prosecution and a counsel for the defense were also chosen. Witnesses were sworn and questioned. The jury deliberated, the judge gave the sentence, and the sheriff carried out his decree.

The first victim at Rich Bar to come before Judge Lynch's court, as the miners' court was called, was a negro named Joshua, who was accused of murdering his employer. Court was held in the El Dorado saloon, and the proceedings were conducted in a very orderly manner. Counsel for the prosecution presented his case, as did the counsel for the defense. The jury brought in a verdict of guilty. The judge pronounced sentence of death, and within a few hours after the trial began, the negro had been officially executed. Eye-witnesses of this execution stated that the negro appeared to be indifferent of his fate. As the sheriff was adjusting the rope, the negro reached into his pocket, took out a plug of tobacco and calmly bit off a "chaw." He was still chewing the tobacco as he swung to a limb. The body was left to hang there until the next morning as an example to the criminally inclined. Then it was taken down and buried.

Beginning with 1851 the United States ran section and township lines at first in the valley and later in the mountains. This work was let by contract at so much a mile. Accordingly it was to the interest of the surveyor to run as many miles as possible. Ten miles of survey a day was customary. No check was made upon the survey. Accordingly when these lines were re-surveyed in later years, wide variances in the surveys were found, occasioning much trouble among landowners.

California's Mother Orange Tree

Bidwell Bar, where gold was first discovered in paying quantities upon the Feather River, also gave to Northern California the Mother Tree of its citrus industry.

This "Mother Orange Tree," as it is known all over California, still thrives at Bidwell Bar. As far as is known it is not only California's oldest but its largest orange tree as well.

The history of this remarkable tree reveals how often the tide of affairs is changed by things considered inconsequential at the time of their happening. The growth of the citrus industry in Northern California, considered in the light of the fact that it sprang from this tree, also reveals the truth of the old axiom that big oaks from little acorns grow.

In the very early Fifties miners brought some oranges to Sacramento. The seeds from one of the oranges were planted in Sacramento in a washtub. Two of the seeds grew.

Judge Lewis, who owned a suspension bridge across the Middle Fork of the Feather River at Bidwell Bar, purchased these two trees. Under his direction they were planted at Bidwell Bar. One of the trees grew and thrived. This was in 1856, and the trees when planted were two years old from the seed.

In 1862 occurred one of the worst floods in the history of the Feather River. The young tree was threatened by the rising waters. Accordingly it was transplanted by Ira R. Ketchum, the keeper of the toll bridge, and taken to higher and safer ground.

The tree is now (1948) ninety-four years of age. It has produced a fine crop of excellent oranges every year, without a single crop failure so far as the record shows.

The immense proportions, considering that it is an orange tree, to which the "Mother Tree" has grown, are shown by some official measurements made in 1923. The height of the tree was 31 feet 6 inches; the average spread of its branches is about thirty feet; the circumference of the trunk a foot above the ground is 5 feet 6 inches.

The miners of the early day were greatly interested in the growth of this tree. It was the first and only orange tree that many of them had seen. Seeds from its fruit were taken to remote cabins and planted there. Today isolated orange trees of the same variety as the Mother Tree are found in many places in the foothills. Sometimes an

The "Mother Orange Tree" at Bidwell Bar, the oldest and largest orange tree in California. The tree is still yielding immense crops of oranges and has never been known to fail to produce a crop.

old fireplace standing near a tree will mark the spot where a miner's cabin once stood. But generally the orange tree is the sole monument that stands to mark the place.

When the mining boom ended, attention was turned to the culture of fruit. And around Oroville attention turned from the gold beneath the ground to that which could be grown on its trees. The adaptability of the foothill section to oranges was established by the fruitful Mother Tree at Bidwell Bar and her numerous progeny of other orange trees scattered over a wide area of foothill country. Accordingly orange planting on a large scale started and in the course of years has become one of the principal industries of the Oroville section.

Dr. H. J. Webber, who was head of the Department of Citriculture of the University of California, had this to say of the historic old orange tree at Bidwell Bar: "The Bidwell Bar orange tree is truly a remarkable specimen. I have examined it personally several times in the last two years and have also studied various seedlings surrounding old miners' cabins in the vicinity grown from seeds that were doubtless taken from the fruit of the Mother Tree. These seedlings are usually productive and in good condition, though they have been neglected for many years and have maintained themselves without manuring, cultivation, or irrigation.

"I examined a group of about a half a dozen of such seedlings at one old cabin last summer that had certainly been neglected for over twenty-five years. Each tree was bearing from a half a box to a box of fruit at the time the trees were examined. This region is mainly covered with forest and has an annual rainfall of from twenty-five to thirty inches. I presume it is this heavy rainfall and the warmth of the region that has assured the success of these neglected trees."

From the Mother Orange Tree at Bidwell Bar, a big commercial orange growing industry has developed in the Oroville District. The oranges from this district are the first to mature in California and are shipped East for the Thanksgiving and Christmas trade. The above view was taken in the Rancho Golden Grove near Oroville.

Notorious Outlaws of the Fifties

While the early mining period in California was characterized by freedom from crime, the latter half of the Fifties was a period of frequent crime, perpetrated often by organized bands of desperadoes, operating under the leadership of outlaws of daring and reckless courage.

The presence of the desperadoes of the latter half of the Fifties is partly to be accounted for by the fact that the lure of California's gold attracted both men of honest ambition and those of criminal ambition to the State.

Again the operations of the Vigilantes in San Francisco caused a general exodus of hard characters from that city into the interior, and the scene of their operations was transferred from San Francisco to the country and particularly to the gold producing sections.

The Feather River diggings were one of the favorite stamping grounds of Tom Bell, one of California's most notorious outlaws during the Fifties.

Bell had been educated to become a physician, but his tastes ran rather to robbery than to medicine, and he abandoned the profession to become the leader of one of the most reckless bands of cutthroats that the country has ever known. From 1855 to 1857 he kept California in a state of terror. Many of his boldest robberies were committed in the Feather River district.

"Rattlesnake Dick," a Canadian, whose real name was never known, also terrorized the Feather settlements from 1856 to 1858. He is described as one of the most desperate outlaws that the State has known.

While there is evidence that members of Joaquin Murietta's gang operated in the mines of the Feather River district, there is no evidence to show that Murietta himself visited this district.

Some time in the year 1858, a desperately hard character appeared in Bangor with his "pal," who was an effeminate youth of jaunty appearance. They appeared to be flush, and for several days held high carnival among the alcoholic spirits of the place.

Finally a man named Fox ferreted them out and charged them with having stopped a priest near Kentucky Ranch and with having relieved him of a three hundred dollar watch that belonged to him, and of $200 that he had collected to aid an orphan asylum. He also announced that the man was Jim Webster, an escaped convict, and that his "pal" was none other than a young damsel, who had attached herself to his precarious fortunes.

The officer was a discreet man. He proceeded to arrest the young woman as she crossed the street alone, but while conversing with her, Webster emerged from a saloon, saw at a glance the turn his affairs had taken, and acted with a promptness born of his experience as a desperado.

As the constable turned to see who was approaching him, he looked into the chambers of a Colt's revolver, not more than six inches away. He was told in tones that did not brook disobedience, to let his prisoner go. He obeyed with alacrity. Webster and his "pal" then left, hand in hand, for the wooded foothills near Bangor.

Several who witnessed the performance fired random shots at the pair, that went wild, but no one assayed to follow in pursuit of the notorious desperado, Jim Webster.

As there were bold outlaws, so there were also daring man hunters.

Steve Vannard, express rider for Wells, Fargo and Company, was once suddenly confronted by three highwaymen, who demanded the express box that he carried. After receiving it, the robbers ordered the driver to go on. Vannard returned to the spot within two hours, and took the robbers' trail. Suddenly the highwaymen arose from behind a log and opened fire. Vannard brought his Winchester into action and killed them all without lowering his rifle from his shoulder. For this he was liberally rewarded by his employers.

It was in the decade of the Seventies, however, that the most notorious of California's outlaws operated in the Feather River district, repeatedly holding up the Oroville-Quincy stage and robbing its treasure box. This desperado was known as Black Bart, and occupies a prominent place in California criminal records. After committing a robbery, it was Black Bart's custom to write a piece of doggerel and leave it at or near the scene of the robbery. In July, 1878, he robbed the Oroville-Quincy stage. Later the treasure box was found by an Indian. In it was the following "poem," which is a fair sample of the verse that Black Bart left as a memento of his crimes:

"Here I lay me down to sleep,
To wait the coming morrow,
Perhaps success, perhaps defeat
And everlasting sorrow.
Yet come what will—I'll try it on,
My condition can't be worse,
And if there's money in that box,
'Tis money in my purse.
"BLACK BART—PO-8."

Black Bart, Charles E. Boles, as it developed his name was, was later captured, a laundry mark on a handkerchief he dropped near the scene of one of his robberies giving the clue that led to his arrest. He was sentenced to serve seven years in the State prison at San Quentin.

He behaved himself well at San Quentin, and was granted the usual credits. So it was that in 1888, less than five years from the date of incarceration, he was released. He stated before leaving the warden's office that it was his intention never again to commit a crime. He was not devoid of wit, for, when one of those present asked him if he was going to write poetry, he answered:

"Didn't you hear me say I would commit no more crimes?"

From San Quentin he went directly to San Francisco, where, with his usual courtesy, he made a friendly call upon the officers who had been instrumental in his capture and conviction.

And then he disappeared, never to be seen or heard of again.

WHEN A GAME OF SEVEN-UP DECIDED A TIE ELECTION

Plumas County was organized in 1854, the territory comprising it being taken from Butte County. In the first election held there to choose county officers, John R. Buckbee and Christopher Porter contested for the office of assessor. The count revealed a tie vote. The law provided that in the event of a tie vote the county judge should make the appointment. Buckbee, the Whig candidate, was a strong personal friend of the then county judge, and it was considered certain that he would receive the appointment. Confronted by this situation, the Democratic friends of Porter proposed that Porter should challenge Buckbee to play a game of seven-up, the winner to be appointed to the office.

The challenge was accepted and the two sat down to the game, surrounded by a big crowd of spectators. Buckbee won the game and the office. However, history records that "the thirsty crowd that witnessed the game reduced the net earnings of Buckbee's office considerably by their liberal potations at his expense."

PROBATING ESTATES

Probating estates was not an involved matter with the early day miners. Daniel Price was killed in a landslide in the early days of Rich Bar. He left ninety-nine ounces of gold. A committee of the representative citizens of the camp was appointed to wind up his estate. They paid all bills and then sent $1800 to the widow. The whole matter was concluded within a week of Price's death.

"Biling" Out of the "Dry" Diggings

While river operations, or "wet" placers, were conducted on a gigantic scale, no less gigantic were operations on the "dry" diggings, as mining operations upon the banks of rivers and streams or upon the flats in their upper reaches were designated by the miners. These grounds were first operated by carrying water to the rockers Then came the "Long Tom" with its continuous stream of water, brought from some dam that had been erected to impound the water. As the miners penetrated back from the streams, the problem of obtaining water became progressively more difficult. Thus is explained the era of ditch digging, colossal in its character and astounding in its extent. To-day all over the hills of the mining district, these ditches are to be found, a monument to the energy of the early miners. In almost every gulch the remnant of a dam is to be found.

Most of these ditches are now useless, but some of the larger of the old mining ditches have been converted into use as irrigation canals.

The most extensive dry diggings were at Forbestown and Oroville. In the dry diggings about Forbestown shafts were sunk in many instances forty or fifty feet to bedrock, where concentrated pay dirt two to four feet in depth was found. This pay dirt was drifted upon and raised by windlass and bucket to the surface where it was washed usually by the rocker and "Long Tom." Much of the territory covered by these dry diggings in the Forbestown mining district yielded from $12,000 to $30,000 an acre. Estimating on the basis of $20,000 to the acre, over $10,000,000 must have been recovered from these diggings alone. The production of placer gold in the entire Forbestown district would be greatly in excess of this amount.

The bluffs and banks of Oroville also were the scene of tremendous mining activity. This activity reached its height in 1856 and 1857. Traces of this activity still remain in the network of tunnels that any considerable excavation on the higher altitudes of Oroville and its suburbs always reveals.

A picture of these operations has been left by the editor of the Butte Record, who, in his issue of August 9, 1856, says: "When the dinner bell rings, the men 'bile' out of the tunnels by the hundreds, and when the turning to time comes they hunt their holes in swarms like the ground squirrels."

Another graphic picture of these diggings is also given in an issue of the North Californian of 1856. We read:

View of "dry" or "bank" diggings. This old picture shows the early methods of mining gold bearing ground that was not located on a stream.

"The stratum of pay dirt is a few hundred feet wide and about two miles long. There are about a thousand men at work on this lead. The amount of labor performed is really astonishing. In many places the pedestrian is compelled to leap over ditches and crawl under sluices at every step. Huge piles of tailings, railways and tail races hem him in on all sides, and he hears nothing but the creaking of horse powers and windlasses and trundling of dirt cars, the ringing of sluice forks and the rattling of boulders."

Oroville's rejoicing at the success of the bluff operations was somewhat tempered by the inundation by water that flowed down on the town from the hill workings.

SPANISH CREEK

Spanish Creek, which the Western Pacific follows for a portion of its course and on which Oakland now maintains a municipal summer vacation camp, takes its name from one of the early landmarks of the Feather River country, Spanish Ranch.

Spanish Ranch in turn was named because of the fact that the first camp established in that section was made by two Mexicans. The same system of nomenclature gave Spanish Peak its title.

This camp was established in 1850. It became a distributing point for surrounding ranches, and at one time boasted of three hotels, with, of course, a corresponding number of saloons.

View of sluices in a tributary of the Feather River. The riffles of the sluice were filled with quicksilver with which the gold amalgamated as it passed over the riffles. The gold found in the Feather River diggings was the finest in the sense of pure gold found in California. The Feather River gold averaged over 900 in fineness and reached 990. The Feather River diggings also were considered the richest in the State, yielding the highest return per man per day of any of the early gold diggings.

Indian Troubles of the Early Days

Clashes between the whites and the Indians were of frequent occurrence during the Fifties, although it was not until the Sixties that the relations between the two reached the stage of mutual retaliatory massacres.

Nor does the evidence indicate that the Indians were wholly to blame for the troubles that early arose between the two races.

In 1854 the residents of Oroville Township, on the north bank of the Feather River, in mass meeting assembled, passed resolutions deploring the attacks "of lawless characters" upon Indian women.

These resolutions recited that the Indians had been driven from their homes and had come to the cabins of miners "with their feet frozen, and nearly famished." The resolutions further declared the intention of the community to lynch the perpetrators of the crimes if they were not summarily dealt with by the courts.

Alonzo Delano tells in his memoirs of the early mining period an incident that occurred upon the Middle Fork of the Feather River in 1850.

Some miners camped upon the Middle Fork missed a number of head of cattle. As it was usual to charge every theft of cattle to the Indians, a party of fifteen men armed themselves and marched to an Indian rancheria, about twelve miles away. There they found a few bones, which they considered proof positive that the Indians had stolen their cattle. They immediately surrounded the Indian campoodie. The Indians seeing the hostile attitude of the whites, tried to escape. The miners opened a fusillade upon them, and fourteen Indians were killed.

After demolishing the huts, the miners started back to their camp, only to find the oxen which they had thought stolen, quietly grazing in a somewhat isolated valley near the camp.

The theft of cattle, the occasional discovery of the body of a miner pierced with Indian arrows, and forays upon a more extensive scale upon the part of mountain Indians, some massacres of Indians in retaliation, all led to an increasing hatred between the races as the decade wore on.

This bitterness culminated in the early Sixties in a number of cruel and atrocious murders of white families by the Indians, particularly by members of the Mill Creek tribe, who were led by a notorious Indian, known to the whites as "Big Foot."

One of the most thrilling incidents of the period and one that led finally to the killing of the entire Mill Creek

ISHI

An Aboriginal Indian whose capture near Oroville in 1911 created a sensation among students of Indian life. University of California savants declared that he belonged to a civilization 20,000 years earlier than that in which he was living. The above picture was taken the morning following his capture.

tribe, men, women and children, was the capture of the Lewis children by the Mill Creeks, the murder of the two little boys, and the subsequent escape of the girl, Thankful Lewis, then but ten years old.

The Lewis family lived on Clear Creek, about ten miles from Oroville.

When returning home from school one day with her two brothers, aged nine and six years old, respectively, the girl, Thankful, and the two boys stopped at Clear Creek to drink from the stream.

As they stood there, Jimmy, the younger brother, suddenly pitched forward dead, as the report of a rifle shot rang out.

Four big Indian bucks, painted with the tribal symbols of war, suddenly emerged from a cluster of trees and

(Continued on Page 36)

CAPTURE OF ISHI, LAST OF DEER CREEKS, A TRUE ABORIGINE

In 1911 there was captured near Oroville an Indian who, until his death, was an object of study by students of Indian lore the nation over and concerning whom a score of books have been written.

For some time meat had been missed at a slaughterhouse on the Oroville-Quincy road. On the evening of August 28, 1911, workmen at the slaughterhouse thought they saw a dog crouching beneath a tree. An investigation revealed that it was an Indian. The man was brought to Oroville and taken to the county jail. He was clad in a piece of canvas that had evidently been discarded by some camper. This was tied together with buckskin thongs.

The appearance of the Indian showed that he was a total stranger to civilization. Electric lights, writing, everything amazed him. Indians were brought to converse with him. Then the mystery deepened. He understood not a single word of their language, nor could they understand a single word that he spoke.

Some months before a surveying party that had been sent into Deer Creek Canyon reported catching a glimpse of wild Indians. Deer Creek was a fastness into which marauding Indians had been driven in the early days of the white settlement. The surmise was hazarded that the Indian captive was the last of the Deer Creeks.

The day following his capture, the Indian was again taken to the slaughterhouse. There by signs he told of a long trip through the mountains. Apparently three Indians had started, two bucks and a mahala. One buck had been shot, evidently being mistaken for a deer by some hunter. His burial was described with vivid signs and loud wailing. The mahala had then died, leaving the one Indian alone.

Indians from every tribe in the vicinity were brought to see the Indian at the county jail, but every attempt to establish communication through language failed.

Stories of the Indian published in the San Francisco press brought Professor Waterman, of the University of California, a student of Indian life, to Oroville. Professor Waterman arrived in a plainly skeptical frame of mind. He was taken to the county jail. For hours Professor Waterman worked there attempting to establish communication with the Indian

(Continued on Page 36)

JAMES P. BECKWOURTH, INDIAN SCOUT
and DISCOVERER *of the* BECKWOURTH PASS

The Beckwourth Pass, through which the Western Pacific passes, is one of the historic passes of the Sierra Nevada Mountains.

Through this pass in the Fifties wound trains of emigrants bound for California over the Beckwourth, or as it was later called, the Beckwith Trail.

The Beckwith Trail follows the ridge of the mountains up the same side of the Feather River as the Western Pacific and paralleling the railroad.

The Beckwourth Trail received its name from James Beckwourth, Indian scout, guide, plainsman, and one of the spectacular pioneer figures of the nation.

Beckwourth was the hero of innumerable adventures and escapades, some of them so extraordinary that their recital by him seriously impaired his reputation for veracity. Historians, however, agree that in the main the story of his life is a true account of a man of reckless daring and courage.

Beckwourth was born in Virginia, apparently in 1798. It seems certain that he had some negro blood in his veins. This gave him enough of the appearance of an Indian to enable him when occasion required it, to pass himself off as an Indian. He became a sub-chief of the Crows, although boasting that he was their head chief.

The story of his elevation to sub-chieftaincy among the Crows is interesting as indicating the character of the man. One of these stories follows:

"A very large grizzly bear had been driven into a cave and Beckwourth asked a great many Crows, who were present, whether any one of them would go in and kill the creature. All declined, for it seemed to be certain death. Beckwourth stripped himself naked, and wrapping a Mexican blanket around his left arm and holding a strong, sharp knife, he entered the cave and after a desperate fight, killed the bear. Beckwourth came out of the cave, all torn and bleeding. He looked like an evil demon, if ever a man did. The Crows were so much pleased at this that he was declared a subject on the spot."

It is related that Beckwourth was once paid a salary of $2000 a year by the United States Government to keep the Crow tribes from molesting the whites as they were crossing the plains. He was employed as a scout by the government on a number of occasions. He was an Indian trader for years.

JAMES P. BECKWOURTH

Finally, after innumerable adventures when about fifty years old, Beckwourth became caught in the stream moving Californiaward, discovered the Beckwourth Pass, and established a stopping place for emigrants near the station now known as Beckwith.

A picture of Beckwourth as he appeared to the emigrants, has been left by Miss Ina Coolbrith, the poet.

The story is told in "Heroes of California," by George Wharton James, as Miss Coolbrith related it to him. He writes concerning the trip of the Coolbrith family over the plains and their meeting with Beckwourth:

"The party had traveled for months over the plains and now, tattered in garments, wearied in body, harassed in mind, sunburned and weatherbeaten, they had reached the place where the plains ended and the steep mountain chain of the Sierras towered before them.

"Indians were dogging their footsteps, and the little girl (Miss Coolbrith) supposed to be asleep in the wagon heard the men talking of the possibility of attack, and there, wide-eyed and full of alarm at danger, the full extent of which she did not understand, she lay and trembled, watching such shadows as were cast, and imagining them the outward signs of the horrors she felt within.

"Then Beckwourth came to their relief. He offered to guide the party through his recently discovered pass to Spanish Ranch, in Plumas County. Well does she remember his coming. A dark faced man, something like a mulatto, with long, braided hair,

reaching down to his shoulders, dressed in beaded buckskin, with moccasins on his feet, and no hat upon his head, he rode into camp. His horse was half saddled, as Indians used to ride in that day. His voice was strong and masterful, but pleasant to the ears of the child, for as soon as he saw that there were children in the train, he took sweetmeats from his pockets and began to distribute them, saying words that cheered the youngsters and made his appearance and dress only the peculiarities of a hero. What a romantic figure he made riding ahead and leading the train, and how happy the little Ina felt to have him, by and by, come to her father's wagon, reach over and lift her up to a place in front of him on his saddle and then go again to the front."

Here is Beckwourth's own story of his discovery of the Beckwourth Pass as related in Bonner's book of his life. He was going from American Valley up to the home of the Pitt River Indians at the time. He says:

"While on this trip I discovered what is now known as Beckwourth Pass in the Sierra Nevada. From some of the elevations over which we passed I remarked away to the southward that seemed lower than any other. I made no mention of it to my companion, but thought that at some future time I would examine into it further.

"After a short stay in the American Valley, I again started out with a prospecting party of twelve men. We killed a bullock before starting and dried the meat. We proceeded in an easterly direction and all busied themselves in searching for gold; but my errand was of a different character. I had come to discover what I suspected to be a pass.

"It was the latter end of April when we entered upon an extensive valley upon the northwest extremity of the Sierra range. The valley was already robed in freshest verdure, contrasting most delightfully with the huge snow-clad masses of rock we had just left. Flowers of every variety and hue spread their variegated charms before us; magpies were chattering and gorgeously plumed birds were caroling in the delights of unmolested solitude. Swarms of wild geese and ducks were swimming on the surface of the cool, crystal stream, which was the central fork of the Rio De Las Plumas (Feather River). Deer and antelope filled the plains, and their boldness was conclusive proof that to them the hunter's

(Continued on Page 20)

The Miners' Ten Commandments

"The Miners' Ten Commandments," printed in California in the first half of the Fifties, were extensively circulated in the gold diggings of California, and from there sent East. The "Ten Commandments" were extensively illustrated with typical mining scenes, the text appearing in the center of the page. These Commandments were:

I.

Thou shalt have no other claim but one.

II.

Thou shalt not make unto thyself any false claim, nor any likeness to a mean man by jumping one.

III.

Thou shalt not go prospecting before thy claim giveth out. Neither shalt thou take the gold dust to the gambling table in vain; for monte, twenty-one, roulette, faro and poker will prove to thee that the more thou puttest down the less thou shalt take up.

IV.

Thou shalt not remember what thy friends do at home on the Sabbath Day; lest the remembrance shall not compare favorably with what thyself doest here. Six days thou mayest dig or pick all that thy body can stand under; but the other day is Sunday; then thou washest all thy dirty shirts, darnest all thy stockings, tap thy boots, mend thy clothing, chop the week's firewood, bake thy bread, that thou wait not when thou returnest from thy long tom weary.

V.

Thou shalt not think more of all thy gold, and how thou canst make it fastest, than how thou will enjoy it after thou has ridden rough-shod over thy good old parents' precepts and examples.

VI.

Thou shalt not kill thy body by working in the rain even if thou shalt make enough to buy physic and attendance with. Neither shalt thou kill thy neighbor's body in a duel; for by keeping cool thou canst save his body and thy conscience. Neither shalt thou destroy thyself by getting "tight," nor "stewed," nor "high," nor "corned," nor "three sheets in the wind."

VII.

Thou shalt not grow discouraged nor think of going home before thou has made thy pile; nor shalt thou grow discouraged because thou has not "struck a lead," nor found a rich crevice, nor struck a hole upon a pocket.

VIII.

Thou shalt not steal a pick, nor a shovel, nor a pan from thy fellow man; nor take away his tools without his leave; nor borrow those he cannot spare.

IX.

Thou shalt not tell any false tales about "good diggings in the mountains" to thy neighbor, that thou mayest benefit a friend who hath mules and provisions and tools and blankets that he cannot sell, lest in deceiving thy neighbor, when he returneth through the snow with naught save his rifle he present thee with the contents thereof.

X.

Thou shalt not commit unsuitable matrimony; nor forget absent maidens; nor neglect thy first love; but thou shalt consider how faithfully and patiently she awaits thy return.

A new commandment I give unto you—if thou hast a wife and little ones that thou lovest dearer than the life—that thou keep them continually before thee to cheer and urge thee onward until thou canst say: "I have enough, God bless them, I will return." Then as thou journeyest toward thy much loved home, with open arms shall they come forth to welcome thee and falling upon thy neck weep tears of unutterable joy that thou art come; then in the fullness of thy heart's gratitude, thou shalt kneel together before thy Heavenly Father to thank Him for thy safe return.

BECKWOURTH, SCOUT AND PATHFINDER—*Continued*

(Continued from Page 19)
rifle was unknown. Nowhere visible were any traces of the white man's approach, and it is probable that our steps were the first that ever marked the spot. This I at once saw would afford the best wagon road into the American Valley."

Beckwourth then tells of his attempts to interest the mining settlements along the route in opening up a wagon road. At Bidwell Bar, he states, "the town was seized with a perfect mania for opening up the route." Substantial aid was promised by Marysville, then the chief outfitting center for the mines. On the strength of this promise, Beckwourth relates that with his own resources he started men at work on the route. He himself went to Truckee to turn the tide of emigration over his route. He became ill with erysipelas. He tells the story through Bonner, as follows: "I was over one hundred miles from medical assistance and my only shelter was a brush tent. I resigned myself to death. However, a train of wagons came up and encamped near where I lay. I was reduced to a very low condition, but I saw the drivers and acquainted them with the object that had brought me out here. They offered to attempt the new road if I thought myself sufficiently strong to guide them through it. The women, God bless them, came to my assistance and through their kind attentions and excellent nursing, I rapidly recovered from my illness. I was soon able to mount a horse and lead the first train, consisting of seventeen wagons, through Beckwourth Pass. We reached the American Valley without the least accident and the emigrants expressed their entire satisfaction with the route. I returned with the train through Marysville and on the intelligence being communicated of the practicability of the route, there was public rejoicing. A northern route had been discovered."

Beckwourth relates that the same night that he arrived in Marysville with his first train, that place was laid in ashes, and he failed, by reason of this calamity, to receive the aid promised. The difference in road building now and then, however, is evidenced by the fact that Beckwourth places his loss, involving his construction outlay, at $1600.

Travel by the Beckwourth route assumed considerable proportions, but slacked in 1855, due chiefly to the construction of the Isthmian Railroad.

Here is one of Beckwourth's stories recounted by Bonner in his "Autobiography of James P. Beckwourth," that accounts in part for the reputation that Beckwourth possessed among early pioneers as being of the lineal line of one Ananias:

"I crossed the stream and when I again appeared in sight of the Indians I was on the summit of a small hill two miles in advance. Giving a general yell they came in pursuit of me. On, on we tore—I to save my scalp and my pursuers to win it.

"At length I reached the Buttes where I had expected to find camp, but, to my inconceivable horror and dismay, my comrades were not there. They had found no water on their route and had proceeded to the river, 45 miles distant.

"On I bounded, following the road our whole company had made. I was scorching with thirst, having tasted neither sup not bite since we began the race. Still I went on with the speed of an antelope. I kept safely in advance of their bullets, when suddenly the glorious sight of the camp smoke caught my eye. My companions soon turned the tables on my pursuers.

"According to the closest calculation I ran that day 95 miles!"

THE GREAT CLIFF U-I-NO; FALLS OF THE FEATHER

In the Grand Gorge of the Middle Fork of the Feather River is the mountain U-I-NO, famous among the Indians of the days before the white man came, as the home of a giant evil spirit.

U-I-NO, more familiarly known among the people today as Bald Rock, is one of the features of a region of the Feather River District which, shunned by the primeval Indians, resisted the efforts of the first white men to explore it or of the miners to prospect it, and today, although one of the most spectacular, is also one of the least known regions of the high Sierras of Northern California.

In this district are the Feather Falls, a stupendous waterfall with a sheer drop of over 500 feet; the Grand Gorge of the Middle Fork of the Feather River, with its great cliff, U-I-NO, which rivals in majesty the famous El Capitan of the Yosemite Valley; the picturesque falls of the Middle Fork of the Feather, the dashing falls of Cascade Creek and Fry Creek, and the entrancing sugar pine forests of the Middle Feather watershed, one of the few virgin pine forests yet left in the Sierras.

The great cliff U-I-NO has a sheer height of 3600 feet. Opposite it is another cliff, nearly perpendicular. Between the two the river is a seething mass of water, which boils, roars and races with tremendous violence.

FEATHER FALLS
One of the most wonderful falls of the Sierras

U-I-NO
The great precipice of the Middle Feather which Indian legend declares was inhabited by an evil giant

The Indians of the primeval period would not go near U-I-NO, and the Indians of the present day are but little less willing. U-I-NO, they believed, was the home of a giant evil spirit. In one part of the Middle Fork Gorge near U-I-NO are great deposits of red dirt. Here, the Indians say that the evil spirit killed great deer and the blood from the deer colored the earth. In another place are two marks, something in the form of the imprint of a knee, but of mammoth dimensions. Here, the Indians believed that the spirit knelt to drink from the waters of the Middle Fork.

The place is one of fearful reverberation in a thunder storm, and the echoes and re-echoes of thunder in the narrow walls of the canyon and against the cliffs are believed to have given rise in the childlike Indian mind to the belief that U-I-NO was the home of an evil spirit of giant size.

U-I-NO towers above the Middle Fork of the Feather River for 3600 feet. It is three-quarters of a mile in length at its base. The mountain is of white granite, and except for a few trees at its top, is absolutely devoid of vegetation.

Through the gorge of the Feather River, a gorge four miles in length, no man was ever known to have passed until the year 1908, when two members of a United States Geological Survey party succeeded in passing through the gorge, but only after a series of escapes from death that were little short of miraculous.

Feather Falls is one of the great waterfalls of the West. It empties into the Middle Fork of the Feather River. The falls themselves have a sheer drop of 500 feet, with 200 additional feet of cascades. For half a mile below the falls the canyon of Fall Creek is filled with a heavy mist. The iridescent lights reflected through the mist are most wonderfully beautiful.

The bottom of the canyon is filled with great granite boulders. The water falling in great masses, roars and booms in a manner that suggests an artillery fire. Looking upwards at the falls themselves, the falling water has the appearance of a cascade of skyrockets.

There are a large number of deep caves and caverns in the canyon. The largest is directly behind the falls.

WHERE GOLD WAS FOUND

An interesting fact in connection with river mining was the absence of values in the deep holes in the river. The biggest recoveries of gold were made from the riffles. One instance will illustrate this. A portion of the West Branch of the North Fork of the Feather River was diverted through a tunnel by a young Englishman who desired to get into two of these river holes which he thought would be filled with gold. The river was diverted and the first of the holes found barren of gold. Before the second hole could be mined, the river rose suddenly over night. The men had left picks, crowbars and other mining equipment there. The water stopped all mining operations for the year. The next year the river was again diverted through the tunnel, and work of mining the second hole was started. Not only was no gold discovered, but none of the heavy iron implements left there the preceding year could be found. Apparently the swirling motion of the water had carried them out of the hole. It is believed that the water kept these holes washed free of gold in the same way.

THE HURDY-GURDY GIRLS

The miners, as a part of their social life, often held stag dances in the bar rooms, the ladies being represented by men with white handkerchiefs tied about their arms. Later the "hurdy-gurdy" girls came. These girls came four together, accompanied by a boy who played the accordion. The dances were held in bar rooms. A dance cost the men fifty cents, one-half of which went to the bar, the other to the girl. These girls traveled on foot from camp to camp, and remained in one camp as long as it was profitable.

Some Songs that the Pioneers Sang

A song that was sung with great glee in the good old days was entitled "Joe Bowers." The author of the song is said to have been a variety actor, John Woodward, who first sang it in San Francisco and later in the mining camps of California. The song spread all over the United States. A number of Pike County people at various times have attempted to find out if there was a real Joe Bowers from Pike County, but their efforts have been without avail, and the question is still an open one. The song was responsible for the erection of a separate building for Pike County at the World's Fair in St. Louis, the only county thus represented.

My name is Joe Bowers,
And I've got a brother, Ike;
I came from old Missouri,
All the way from Pike.
I'll tell you why I left there
And how I came to roam,
And leave my poor old Mammy,
So far away from home.

I used to love a gal there—
Her name was Sally Black;
I axed her to marry me,
She said it was a whack.
Says she to me, "Joe Bowers,
Before we hitch for life
You ought to get a little home
To keep your little wife."

"O, Sally, dearest Sally,
O Sally, for your sake,
I'll go to California
And try to raise a stake."
Says she to me, "Joe Bowers,
You are the chap to win:
Here's a kiss to bind the bargain,"
And she hove in a dozen in.

* * * *

At length I went to mining,
Put in my biggest licks,
Went down upon the boulders,
Just like a thousand bricks;
I worked both late and early,
In rain, in sun, in snow;
I was working for my Sally—
It was all the same to Joe.

I made a lucky strike
As the gold itself did tell,
I saved it for my Sally—
The gal that I loved so well—
That on my return to Pike
I might pour it at her feet,
And she would hug and kiss me
And call me something sweet.

At length I got a letter
From my dear brother, Ike,
It came from old Missouri,
All the way from Pike.
It brought me the darndest news
That ever you did hear—
My heart is almost bursting
So pray excuse this tear.

It said that Sally was false to me,
Her love for me had fled;
She got married to a butcher—
The butcher's hair was red;
And more than that the letter said
(It's enough to make you swear)
That Sally has a baby, and
The baby has red hair.

ARTICLES IN A MINER'S CREED

Entered according to Act of Congress in the year 1855, by James M. Hutchings in the Clerk's Office of the District Court for Northern District of California.

He believes in fifty cents to the pan and the bedrock "pitching."

He believes in the top dirt paying wages and water money; and the bottom dirt—a fortune.

He believes that sheets in hotels should not be considered clean after five weeks' use without washing.

He believes that a good Sunday dinner is not hard to take after a week's work and fasting on flapjacks and molasses.

He believes that butter sent to the mines should not be used as motive power—although strong enough for anything.

He believes in big vegetables, because he sees them; but wonders if there is any other kind of fruit than dried apples scalded, and dried apples with the strings in.

In the first half of the Fifties, "The California Emigrant" was one of the favorite songs of the mining camps. Jonathan Nichols is given as the author. It was sung to the tune of "Oh, Susannah." The words follow:

I came from Salem City
With my washbowl on my knee;
I'm going to California,
The gold dust for to see.

Chorus:
Oh, California!
That's the land for me,
I'm going to Sacramento
With my washbowl on my knee.

It rained all night the day I left,
The weather being dry,
The sun so hot I froze to death—
Oh, brothers, don't you cry.

I jumped on board the Liza ship
And traveled on the sea;
And every time I thought of home,
I wished it wasn't me.

The vessel reared like any horse,
That's had of oats a wealth,
It found it couldn't throw me—so
I thought I'd throw myself.

I soon shall be in Francisco,
And then I'll look around;
And when I see the gold lumps there,
I'll pick them off the ground.

I'll scrape the mountains clean, my boys,
I'll drain the river dry,
A pocket full of rocks bring home—
So brothers, don't you cry.

He believes that hash set upon the table twice a day for two weeks, after that should be considered pickles.

He believes that gold is found in quartz, but he would be satisfied to find it in pints—or even half pints.

He believes that nine persons sleeping in one room, only twelve by ten, should not allow the landlord to double the number—at the same charge.

He believes that man to be a knave who foolishly squanders his earnings here, and allows his wife and children to be starving at home.

He believes that with gentle hands to aid him, gentle words to cheer him, and gentle smiles to welcome him, he could enjoy life as it passes and work hard and willingly until fortune should crown his labors with success—for

He believes that California, with all its social drawbacks, is not only a great country, but that it is in every sense the best place in the world for a working man, and only waits the coming of a good, sensible and intelligent and contented class of noble-minded women to make "the desert bloom as the rose," and man to be rich, contented and happy.

So mote it be.

FORTY NINE.

The Lava Beds Excitement

During the Sixties mining lagged in the Feather Diggings, but in the following decade it became both active and spectacular.

It was during the decade of the Seventies that the so-called "Lava Beds" excitement at Oroville reached its culmination. The same decade also saw its decline.

The Lava Beds, as they were called, a district near Oroville, were mined by Chinese. By 1872 the operations of the Chinese there had attracted the attention of California's celestial population and Chinese by the hundreds

The newspapers of the decade give accounts of continuous conflicts between the Chinese and the members of the white race.

The Chinese were frequently robbed of their gold dust by bands of white bandits. The Chinese, however, were not always the innocent victims of white wrong-doing. As early as 1871, a gang of twelve Chinamen were traced to a cave in a bluff at Oroville, where they were arrested. The entrance to the cave was a hole barely large enough for a man to crawl

tax collector and instantly the hand of justice descends upon his puny head. Let but the slightest shadow of a pigtail be seen behind a manzanita bush and 40,000 sheriffs and constables are seen rushing to and fro in hot haste and their zeal never flags until John has paid his six dollars a month; but now that one of them has been murdered in cold blood, there has not been so much as an inquiry concerning the matter made by any officer of the law."

The Butte Record, also published in Oroville, throws an illuminating sidelight upon justice as it was not accorded the Chinese. Says that paper in its issue of August 29, 1856:

"One of those old-fashioned gatherings of miners to hang somebody came off yesterday at the bluff, just above town. A Chinaman spoken of in connection with a robbery of $100, was the victim. He protested his innocence. The loser of the money, headed by a great crowd, fastened the fatal rope around his neck and with one end fastened to the windlass, was about to let him drop into a shaft when two deputy sheriffs arrived just in time to spoil all their wicked fun by arresting the Chinese. The evidence indicates he is innocent."

The above picture, taken from an old oil painting, shows Chinese methods of mining in the Feather River Diggings. The picture shows in the foreground a Chinaman standing by the rocker pouring water upon the gravel within the rocker. His companions are working below him bringing the pay dirt up to the rocker.

rushed to Oroville. In 1874 Oroville was said to have had a Chinese population of 10,000, and to be the largest Chinese settlement in California, outside of San Francisco.

The Chinese were brought to Oroville by special trains. These trains were met at the depot by police officials, who marched the Chinese to the Court House Square, where their poll tax was collected. The Chinese were then free to go where they pleased.

The Chinese operated the ground by sinking shafts to depths of 30, 40 and 50 feet. Men were enabled to work at the bottom of these shafts through the fact that pumps were operated continuously, keeping them free from water. The gravel from the bottom of the shafts was shoveled into tubs, which were carried by windlasses to the surface of the ground. There the gravel was dumped into wheelbarrows and wheeled to nearby reservoirs to be washed. In each of these reservoirs were a number of Chinamen who shoveled the wet dirt into old fashioned rockers. On the side of the rocker stood a patriarchal Chinaman, rocking away as solicitously as a mother would rock her child. At night each rocker was cleaned up and the "head man" took charge of the gold.

through. The cave itself was found literally filled with loot stolen by the Chinese.

The Lava Beds excitement reached its climax in the latter half of the Seventies. In 1878 the excitement was largely over. It was reported that the Chinese population of Oroville in that year had decreased to 2000 persons.

BE-DEVILING THE CHINESE

Increasing numbers of Chinese in the gold diggings was one of the principal causes of infractions of the peace among the miners.

In 1852, a tax in the nature of a license fee was imposed on all foreigners operating in the mines. The collection of this tax was chiefly confined to the Chinese.

The North Californian of Oroville, in its issue of December 1st, 1855, gives a contemporaneous glimpse of the attitude of the miners of the Fifties toward the Chinese. We read:

"One of the Chinamen who was robbed and injured a few days ago near Oroville, is dead. Not even by word, look, or deed, has this community expressed the slightest displeasure at this unprovoked murder. Let a Chinaman be guilty of the heinous crime of not having enough to pay the

PIONEER COOKERY

Harry C. Peterson, a well-known student of early California life, quotes "an old timer" as follows on the subject of pioneer cooking:

"We all had to do our own cooking; sometimes we took turns at it, but a fellow never showed off his ability but once. After that he found himself hectored to death to do the other fellow's cooking while they were digging out the nuggets.

"I didn't have anything but my frying pan and big iron bean kettle for my cooking, except my bowie-knife. The frying pan I used for bacon and flapjacks. By frying bacon first, I had a nice greasy pan ready to fry my flapjacks in. Flapjacks ranked all the way from nice tender ones right on up to rawhides. We used to get yeast in little tin cans, powdered. This we used with the flour and dried milk when we could afford it. When we couldn't we just mixed up flour and water and a little salt and fried 'em. After they had been smeared with bacon grease right plentifully, you couldn't tell whether they had been made of yeast cake or sawdust.

"The bean pot was always partly full of beans. On Sunday we put on a full pot of Chili beans to cook. They were dandy beans, too. By morning they were done, and we had enough to last till Thursday night.

"Our coffee was made of everything but coffee beans. They used to roast dried peas and old wheat, grind them up, and sell it to us for coffee."

A Water Well That Proved a Gold Bonanza

The history of mining in the Feather River District is by no means confined to the "Days of Old, the Days of Gold, the Days of '49."

Just as the sluice followed the rocker and the flume the long tom, so improved methods of finding gold were developed with succeeding decades of gold mining activity.

The era of hydraulic mining of the Seventies and Eighties marked one of the steps forward in mining methods. The mining industry, however, found its culminating success in the development of gold mining by the dredging method, the birth place and cradle of which were Oroville.

It is interesting as showing in what small things great industries are sometimes conceived, that the dredging industry which has added millions of dollars to the world's wealth had its beginning when W. P. Hammon, a nurseryman on the Feather River bottom lands, stood watching the progress of a well that he was having dug upon his land. From the dirt thrown out he picked tiny flecks of gold. The thought occurred to him that there should be some commercial way of recovering this gold. From this thought came the gold dredging industry, that in two decades spread from Oroville about the world, that has enormously increased the world's supply of gold, and made Mr. Hammon one of the outstanding figures in the history of mining and one of the major factors in the development of California.

These great "gold boats," as they have been called, are constructed in pits, which after the dredgers are built, are filled with water. The gold boat digs its way forward by continuous buckets and as it goes it carries its pond with it. The buckets dump their load of precious gravel into a trommel where the gravel is washed. The fine stuff is carried over a series of riffles, which catch the gold in quicksilver. The debris and rocks are disposed of by means of long stackers, forming the "tailings piles" so characteristic of a gold dredging section.

It is an interesting fact that following in the wake of the gold dredgers came rock crushers, and the boulders forming the tailings piles are being manufactured into crushed rock. This crushed rock has gone to ballast California's railroads, to make concrete for California's wonderful system of highways, and into building operations generally. Today the crushed rock industry of Northern California depends largely for its supply of material upon the tailings piles of the gold dredger fields.

Not the least interesting phase of the gold dredging industry has been the fact that the land after being level-ed by rock crusher or for other purposes has been replanted to fruit. Some of the earliest and best fruit grown in California comes from this dredged land.

Since gold dredging is usually confined to waste river land, adjacent to flowing streams, their operations are

An Oroville Fig Orchard growing on land from which the gold had been taken by gold dredging operations.

frequently under the control of Army Engineers, whose duty it is to regulate stream flow. The dredging companies of California, particularly along the Yuba River, near Hammonton, have fully co-operated with the War Department Engineers in providing flood control levees and otherwise regulating the flow of streams, so that the agricultural interests of nearby valleys have benefitted without being obliged to expend large sums for building levees. As the great fleet of gold boats on the Yuba River dug the gold from the ground, the tailings were so deposited that the debris in the river channel was restrained and flood protection walls built out of the tailings piles.

Again the gold taken from the ground by the gold dredgers has been one of the great factors in the general development of Northern California. This gold has gone into the development of irrigation, power and all the resources of the State.

The Natomas Company of California, operating gold dredgers in the Oroville field on the Feather River and the Folsom field on the American River, has reclaimed 90,000 acres of this land north of Sacramento. Into the reclamation of this land, now one of the finest belts of agricultural land on the market, over $6,000,000 has gone.

The huge scale on which the gold dredgers operate makes it possible to handle ground at a cost as low as four cents per cubic yard. Despite the low operating costs, however, the area capable of dredging in California is limited. Ground offering promise of profit is only found where a torrential stream, traversing gold-bearing formations, debouches

upon a valley. There it deposits its burden of gold. But it is further necessary, to make dredging for gold profitable, that the boulders be not too large and that the gravel be capable of being washed clean of dirt, so that gold is not carried in clay or dirt over the riffles, designed and capable only of catching free gold.

The era of gold dredging on the Feather River is largely gone. But two gold boats were operating in 1924, as against a fleet of forty of these dredgers a decade ago. But the industry must not be judged by the tailings piles it has left behind it.

The strangers in passing through a gold dredging field should see in these tailings not merely piles of boulders, but rather miles of good roads now being built and yet to be built from them; orchards planted in the wake of the dredger upon the very ground that has been dredged of its gold; railroads made safe by ballasting obtained from these tailings; monumental buildings constructed from concrete, the rock for which was made available by gold dredging operations; electric roads constructed from the gold the dredgers recovered; flooded and swamp land made into fertile agricultural fields with gold the dredging industry yielded. These things have been the real legacy of the industry to California, and a rich legacy it has been indeed.

The accompanying picture is that of a gold dredger which operated in the Oroville district. The boat floats in a pond that it digs as it goes. The ground is dug by means of a continuous bucket line, the cutting lip of the bucket being made of the best manganese steel. The buckets dump their load into a hopper, where the dirt is washed by a continuous stream of water playing upon it, and where the stones are separated from the dirt. The dirt then goes over the sluices, where the gold is caught in riffles filled with quicksilver. The rock and dirt from which the gold has been taken are dumped from the rear of the "gold boat," forming the tailings piles characteristic of a field that has been mined by the gold dredger process.

An Oroville "Gold Boat"

Mining With Monitors

View of Hydraulic Mining Operations at Cherokee near Oroville

Hydraulic mining in the Feather River District reached its climax, however, in the Eighties, when the Feather River area boasted of the most completely equipped hydraulic mine in the world.

This mine was at Cherokee, twelve miles from Oroville. In 1880 this mine was equipped with eighteen hydraulic monitors, throwing streams of water nine inches in diameter. It had nine miles of gold-saving sluices. Debris was cared for by distributing it over 21,000 acres of valley land, purchased by the company for that purpose. Other equipment was on a similar scale. The recovery of gold ran far into the millions.

While this was the largest hydraulic mine, many other properties at Oroville and in other parts of the county were operated by the hydraulic method. Many of these mines were closed down when valley farmers instituted proceedings to stop hydraulicking because of the fact that the debris from the mines was filling the rivers and causing the inundation of their lands with debris from the mines.

BOOSTING AMONG CALIFORNIANS AN INHERITED ART

The perusal of the early papers shows that boosting is an inherited art with Californians and dates back to the beginning of things in this State. Thus in 1856, Oroville was the fifth city in point of size in California. Commenting on this fact the editor of the North Californian delivered himself as follows in one of the issues of his paper:

"One year ago Oroville consisted of only a few dozen houses and a few hundred idle men. At that time we predicted that Oroville would become the most important mining town in the State. We prophesied that Table Mountain would be found to contain extensive gold deposits. We talked of our coal fields and of the quartz leads in the vicinity. We said Oroville would be the county seat; it would have a steamboat and in two or three years would have a railroad and would command the trade of Butte and Yuba Counties. We were charged with trying to maintain by exaggerated statements, the fortunes of a mushroom town. One San Francisco paper called us the 'Oroville Trombone'; another made merry over our visions of steamboats, railroads, coal mines, etc. We can only point to our mines, our steamboat, which is almost in sight, our coal yard, our splendid courthouse, our 1700 votes, our brilliant prospects, and quote the old adage, 'The proof of the pudding is in chewing the bagstrings.'"

Where surface gold was as plentiful as it was in the very early period on the Feather River diggings, the necessity for hydraulic mining did not exist. Accordingly in the early Fifties there is only a trace of the most primitive methods of hydraulic mining. In May, 1854, the Butte Record comments as follows on this form of mining:

"We notice on several of the bank claims in this vicinity, miners have introduced hose pipe, where water can be raised to a sufficient height to give it force. Some of them appear to throw a stream with nearly the force of a fire engine. This stream directed against a bank of solid earth and stone, wears it away with astonishing rapidity, and after rendering the dirt in the best possible condition, carries it down through the sluice."

The above picture is of the famous "Bracket Flume," built during the days when hydraulic mining was at its height, to bring water for hydraulic operations to Oroville. The flume was hung on the face of a basalt cliff of Table Mountain, opposite Oroville, by brackets. The height of this basalt cliff is 325 feet. Back of the flume can be seen one of the wonderful Table Mountain waterfalls.

HOW THE MINERS GOT THEIR MAIL

A monument should be erected to the memory of the mountain express messengers of the Fifties. A keen sense of duty compelled them to brave perils before which the bravest might well quail. They did their duty as a matter of course. In winter, as well as in summer, they covered their routes. If a mountain settlement was not reached, it was because the task was impossible.

Captain Singer was one of the best known of these mountain express messengers. How many heroic deeds and brave marches, how many. perils braved, how many hearts comforted with news from home, can be read between the lines of an obscure item that appeared in the Butte Record of January 21, 1854: "Captain Singer for the first time in his life failed to get farther than the Mountain House in consequence of the snow. He returned the second day." And again in the issue of February 18th of the same year, we find further evidence of the devotion of Captain Singer to his duty. We read: "That intrepid and untiring mountain expressman, Captain Singer, has been perambulating the mountains during the recent snow storm. He was, of course, obliged to traverse huge mountains of snow, before which the heart of any other man would have sunk in despair. But the Captain never surrenders. His last trip used up three pairs of boots besides innumerable snow shoes. He deserves great credit for his untiring efforts to furnish the mountain boys with news from the regions of mud below."

Another famous express was that of Whiting and Company. In 1858 Fenton B. Whiting, head of the company, started a dog express service over the mountains. He secured three dogs of the Newfoundland and St. Bernard breeds and these he broke to harness. The first trip was a magnificent success. On the sled was a small chest in which were carried the mail and express packages. This, with Mr. Whiting and an occasional passenger, made a load of fully six hundred pounds. With this load the dogs would race across the snow. The dog express continued in service until the introduction of snow shoes on horses, in 1865, when the dog express gave way even in winter to the stage service.

The rivalry between Wells, Fargo and Company and Adams and Company, the two major express companies, was very keen.

In 1853-54 a race took place up through the northern counties between the two companies that furnished a topic for conversation among the miners for years. W. S. Lowden, one of the participants in the race, tells the story as follows:

"Great preparations were made for the race. Every known fast horse along the route was pressed into service, and very naturally the best known riders were in demand. As high as $100 was paid to the owners of horses for the privilege of riding them from three to five miles. Horses were placed about four miles apart by each company. Every animal had

a man to care for it, who was also provided with an extra horse to ride himself. Both relays of horses were kept under saddle from December 28th, 1853, to January 3, 1854."

The uncertainty of the time that the race was to start was due to the fact that the messengers were to carry the President's message from San Francisco to Portland, Oregon, and it was not known at what hour or moment the steamer might arrive in San Francisco with the text of the President's message on board.

Lowden continues his story as follows: "The race was very close from San Francisco to Tehama. Wells, Fargo and Company led at Marysville. Between Marysville and Tehama, Adams and Company's messenger passed the Wells, Fargo rider, and the Mexican who took the bags

from him reached the river first and crossed to the Tehama side just as Wells, Fargo and Company's reached the opposite bank and jumped into a boat. Here my race commenced. I sprang into the saddle with the bags, which weighed fifty-four pounds. I changed horses nineteen times between Tehama and Shasta, touching the ground but once. That was at Prairie House, where Tom Flynn, the man in charge of my horse, was engaged in a fight with the keeper of the Wells, Fargo and Company's horse, and had let mine get loose. I saw the situation at a glance, rode my tired horse a little past the place where the fight was going on, sprang to the ground, caught the fresh horse by the tail as he was running away from me and went into the saddle over his rump at a single bound. Turning to the horse I had just left with the express bags, I pulled them over on my fresh horse and renewed the race. I lost about one minute here. All other changes I made while the horses were running, the keeper leading the horse I was to ride, and riding his extra horse. I would make myself heard with a whistle about a half mile before reaching the change, which gave ample time to tighten the cinch and start the fresh horse on the road. When I reached him, the keeper would have my horse in a lively gallop, and I sprang from one horse to the other as they moved."

The race was won by Adams and Company.

THE HUNGER FOR HOME MAIL

The arrival of the mail was one of the big events of the week in the mining camps. The local newspapers chronicled it as one of the chief features of the issue. The delight of those who received letters from home and the disappointment of those who failed to receive such letters were duly set forth.

The inadequacy of the mail service was partly compensated for by an exceptionally thorough-going and efficient express service. The compensation received by the expressman was one dollar for each letter delivered and half that amount for newspapers.

Harry C. Peterson in his interesting accounts of early day life, calls attention to the human wreckage that the faulty mail service caused. He writes: "Thousands of lives were ruined because letters failed to reach Frank, Bill or Tom just at the critical stage, that stage of homesickness where the world went black and the door of a saloon looked like the pearly gates of heaven."

Perils the Pioneers Braved

The winter of 1852-53 in the mountainous area along the Feather River was one of terrific severity. The storms set in unusually early, and caught many of the merchants without their usual stocks of provisions on hand.

The severest storm of the winter occurred between Christmas and New

The Prospector

Year's Day. It continued for several days following the latter date.

Pack trains were brought by almost superhuman efforts to points as near the mountain mining settlements as they could reach. From there provisions were packed in by men upon their backs.

The mules in one pack train refused to go over the top of a mountain where the wind had piled the snow along a high bluff. The mules were blindfolded, led to the top of the bluff and pushed over. The animals rolled with their packs to the waiting miners in the ravine below. Such measures had to be adopted to save the miners from starvation.

In December, 1852, the miners at Rich Bar, on the North Fork of the Feather River, faced the alternative of either fighting their way to an outside settlement or starving.

A band of seventy men left Rich Bar on December 28th, headed for Bidwell Bar. The group included Americans, Frenchmen, Mexicans, Kanakas and one Chinaman. They took turns in leading the line and wallowing their way through the snow, that a path might be made for the others to follow. Foot by foot, and yard by yard, they fought their way forward. Several became so exhausted that they were unable to proceed. These perished in the snow. At the top of the mountain, a deserted cabin was found. Here the party stayed that night, all crowding within its narrow walls. Early the next morning the men began their march again. Another day's march brought them to Spanish Ranch where food and fire were had.

Almost on the same day, a party of four men left Soda Bar. They had gone but a few miles when the severity of the storm increased. The men were but scantily clothed. None of them had a full suit of clothes. One of them wore but boots, pants, hat, and a woolen shirt from which the buttons had been torn.

When the men reached Frenchmen's Hill, they found that their trail was fast being obliterated by the snow. They walked four abreast, so that the judgment of all was available in locating the trail. Soon they discovered that they had left the trail. They started back, only to lose the trail time after time. The last time that the trail was lost found them at an old pine stump, the hollow part of which was filled with pitch. This they knew would burn all night and save them from freezing. But their matches were wet and they could not light the stump.

The men forced their way on and finally came to a brook running in a narrow channel between walls of snow at least twenty feet deep. These walls had been banked up by the wind. Into this brook the men descended. The water was less than a foot deep, but it was warmer than the snow, and the snow walls gave them some protection against the biting blast of the winter gale.

Here they waded back and forth, back and forth, hour after hour, in a desperate attempt to keep blood circulating in their veins. One of them, the most poorly clad of the four, could make no further effort. His companions made a bench in the snow, and taking turns, one with the other, they held their disabled companion in their arms until death finally relieved his suffering.

Finally dawn appeared. But the only one of the party who pretended to have any knowledge of the country was dead.

Taking the pistol and gold dust from the body of their dead companion, the three men again started forward.

After struggling for hours, the men

Sacramento in 1849

chanced across a blazed tree, and then another, and another. They were on a trail, leading to some settlement somewhere. However, before they reached the settlement, night again came upon them. All night long the three men paced back and forth on a path between two trees. Again the morning broke and once more they took up their march. The blazed trail finally led them into Peavine, a mountain hotel on the Oroville-Quincy road, where succor and warmth were provided.

The men rested a few days and then beat their way through the snow back to the brook where their companion had died. There they gave

Rudely constructed fireplaces scattered over the Feather River District are monuments to the "Days of Old."

his body a Christian burial. Then they continued on their way to Oroville, where the gold dust of the dead man was deposited in a bank to the credit of his partner.

"RICH" RICH BAR

(Continued from Page 10)

childbirth, that in 1915 the Grand Parlor of the Native Sons of the Golden West dedicated the monument that stands above the Western Pacific tracks.

Provisions were brought into the camp by packers in trains of from fifty to one hundred burros and mules. Everything sold for $1 a pound, except flour, which brought $1.50.

A glimpse of life at Rich Bar when it was in its heyday is contained in the reminiscences of U. S. Dean, who went there in 1851, when he was twenty-one years old. "Life at Rich Bar was at its height in 1852 and 1853," he writes. "Fully 2500 lived on the flat and on the hillsides at that time. The houses for the most part consisted of log cabins There were also a good many tents.

"The saloons were always crowded. Gold dust was measured out for the drinks. No change was given or expected. Everybody had money or at least gold dust. Gambling was wide open and everything went. The stakes were big.

"Dances were held every now and then. A troupe of women would travel through the mountains from one mining camp to the other and stage dances."

In 1858 Rich Bar began to decline.

Banking in the Pine Trees; "Busted" by the Squirrels

While drinking and gambling flourished among the miners from the earliest period, all accounts agree upon the comparative infrequence of theft in 1849.

Gold was left in pans and rockers while the miners went to their meals, and gold remained safe and untouched in their canvas tents while the miners were away at work on their claims.

Judge C. F. Lott, who came to California in 1849, in reminiscences of that period, states that on one occasion, in company with others, he saw a pan with at least $1000 in gold dust near the trail along which they were riding, and in plain view of the trail. Nearly a week later he passed by the place for a second time, and the pan with its contents of gold dust remained untouched, although many men had passed along the trail during the week.

In fact, the attempt to conceal the gold was more perilous than when it was left exposed to the public view, as is witnessed by the amusing experience of one miner in the Berry Creek section. The Butte Record tells the story as follows:

"A hombre who has been in the employ of the Berry Creek Mill Company during the past year, buried some $500 for safe keeping. Having recently to use his change, he went to his place of deposit, but could not find his money. The squirrels had struck a pocket and being prudent creatures, had made a division and removed it to various holes and hiding places in sums to suit their idea of wealth and importance. One avaricious old rascal had deposited $200 in one place, placing it all up edgewise with the greatest care.

"After about two weeks' search the owner succeeded in finding $340 of the original $500 and then sold the claim for $30 to some lucky hombre, who had discovered another deposit. Perhaps he will hereafter heed the practical lesson given by the squirrels, and keep his money in circulation."

It was not unusual for the early miners to make a safe of some tree near their claim. One of these was discovered near Bangor in 1892. A woodchopper there was cutting down trees for firewood. He noticed a peculiar scar on one of the trees, and having heard that the early miners sometimes cached their treasure in trees, he carefully cut into the pine.

He found an old hole in the tree that had been overgrown with bark. Within this hole was a tin box filled with gold dust and nuggets.

A general prospecting of the trees of that neighborhood followed, but without results.

CALIFORNIA CURRENCY

During the period before the discovery of gold, trade in California was chiefly conducted by barter. In 1849 and the early period of the Fifties, the principal medium of exchange was gold dust. This remained true of the more remote mining settlements throughout the whole decade of the Fifties.

There were also in circulation privately minted coins of octagonal shape, made in San Francisco. These were the "slugs" of mining parlance. These were in ten, twenty and fifty dollar denominations. They were octagonal shaped gold coins, made out of unalloyed soft gold. After 1853 many Spanish and English coins found their way into the currency of the section, as well as some Mexican money. Gold dust, however, was still extensively used. In the latter half of the decade coins of the United States minting became more plentiful.

In 1854 complaint was made in the newspapers that San Franciscans were tampering with the California coinage, and either filing $6 or $7 worth of gold from the slugs or boring into the gold pieces, extracting the gold, and filling the hole with lead and gilding it over. In the latter part of 1856 the bankers of San Francisco offered to receive the California coin at weight, allowing $18.25 per ounce. This had the effect of rapidly retiring the private currency.

WHEN COURTS MADE THEIR OWN PRECEDENTS

(Continued from Page 11)

that a decision in favor of the plaintiff would thus be certain to bring the needed fees. The defendant refused to give the bonds. A big crowd was witnessing the trial and became highly indignant at Bonner's demand. A meeting was called and a committee appointed to demand that Bonner adjourn court.

Bonner refused and a formal order was again made in the name of the people that he adjourn court. It was supper time and the worthy judge took advantage of the hour to adjourn court until the next morning; but before the morning arrived he left camp astride the hurricane deck of a patient pack mule. He had a place in Onion Valley many feet higher than the mining camps, which he called his "higher court." Here he continued the case without the presence of the defendant, and gave judgment to the plaintiff in order to collect his fees.

This is but one of a number of similar stories that are told of the manner that the peregrinating justice administered the duties of his office.

The records tell of shootings in court, and it was the common thing for attorneys, the Court and for court officials to come into the court room "heeled" with pistols and revolvers. In early litigation, particularly over mining claims, possession was nine points of the law and a goodly part of the tenth point. The application of this rule not infrequently led to violence, both in the courts and elsewhere.

The Feather River Canyon constitutes the principal copper producing section of California.

The above view is that of the first bank established in Oroville. Banking during the Fifties was not so much a matter of loaning money as of buying gold dust and nuggets. On Sunday the miners would come into town and a long line would form before the bank, each miner bringing in his clean-up to be weighed and sold. As an incidental matter to buying gold dust, money was loaned at the modest sum of five per cent interest per month

E CLAMPUS VITUS, THE MINERS' FAVORITE FRATERNAL ORDER

The color and uniqueness of California life in the period of the State's most romantic history was reflected in a fraternal organization, "E Clampus Vitus," whose branches extended through all mining camps of the State.

Thomas E. Farish, in his book, "The Gold Hunters of California," tells the story of this most distinctive and spectacular order. He writes:

"Lawyers, bankers, merchants, miners, were members of E Clampus Vitus; and when the hew gag, a big horn, rang out, from miles around miners came; stores and banks were quickly closed and all their managers speedily repaired to the Clampus hall.

"A candidate was prepared for the initiation by being divested of most of his clothing and then blindfolded. In this condition he was led around the hall, stopping at different points, where he was catechized and lectured in a most fatherly way by the different officers of the lodge.

"About the time he became worked up to the solemnity of the occasion, a strap with a ring attached, was suddenly placed about his body and he found himself suddenly lifted to the ceiling, and then as suddenly dropped into a wheelbarrow, purposely prepared for the reception. In this wheelbarrow large sponges, saturated with water, had been placed.

"The victim would be held there securely while the wheelbarrow was run around for a couple of hundred feet, or more, over a rough construction of round poles, jolting the wheelbarrow and keeping the victim bobbing up and down on his ice cold cushions in a most ridiculous manner.

"During the performance, the members of the order sang the while: 'Ain't you glad to get out of the wilderness, get out of the wilderness, get out of the wilderness,' and so on indefinitely.

"Sometimes these initiation ceremonies extended over several hours. By the time they got through with a candidate, the new member would feel certain that he had paid well for the entertainment of his friends.

"Invariably the new member would steal out of town, humiliated and crestfallen, to appear again only when he could produce some new candidate or victim for admission to the order."

The first marriage license granted in Butte County was in 1862. Previous to that time marriages had been celebrated without necessity of a license. The first couple to be granted a wedding license in Butte County were a Chinese couple, Quin Choo and Lun Hee, both of Oroville.

THE FIRST MASONIC MEETING

In the fall of 1849, a Mr. Norse called all members of the Masonic order together who were then living at Long Bar, near Oroville. The meeting was called under a dispensation of the Grand Lodge of Illinois, of which

California's oldest Masonic Hall. This hall, at Forbestown, was built in 1855 and has been used continuously as a meeting place of the Forbestown Masonic Lodge since 1860.

Norse was a member. This is said to be the first Masonic meeting held in California. The convocation was held in a shake shanty with walls so thin that the tyler was forced to exercise special diligence to see that the secrets of the order did not "leak out." No lodge was chartered.

Where the Sacramento's waters roll
   their golden tide along,
Which echoes through the mountains
   like a merry drinking song;
Where the Sierra Nevada lifts its
   crests unto the sky,
A home for freedom's eagles when the
   tempest's sweeping by;

Where the Bay of San Francisco—the
   Naples of the West—
Lies sleeping like an infant beside the
   ocean's breast;
There we go with dauntless spirits,
   and we go with hearts elate,
To build another empire—to found an-
   other State.

—Stanzas of song widely sung in '49 and '50 throughout the Eastern States.

The old jail at Bidwell Bar as the building now appears. The jail is now the property of the Bidwell Bar Park Association, and it is proposed to convert the structure into a museum where relics of pioneer days will be gathered and displayed.

FIRST FOURTH OF JULY CELEBRATION ON THE FEATHER

Miners of the Feather River diggings celebrated the Fourth of July in 1850 at a celebration given at Ophir, now Oroville. It was the first Fourth of July celebration to be held north of Sacramento.

The celebration, as the day wore on, developed into even a more exciting affair than those who had planned the program had intended.

The story is told by Wells and Chambers in an early history of Butte County. We quote as follows:

Great preparations had been made for a grand celebration. The stalled ox was slain to adorn a barbecue. C. F. Lott, a promising young attorney, was selected as a fit person to read the Declaration of Independence.

"The day dawned beautifully, being ushered in with the customary noisy salutes. Ere long the miners from the neighboring camps began to assemble. The only ladies present were Mrs. Tatham and a Miss Brown from Thompsons Flat. She, being unmarried, was the belle of the day.

"At the appointed time, Mr. Lott rose and read, amidst the closest attention of his hearers, the inspiring words of the Declaration of Independence.

"To one of his hearers the language seemed fresh and original. This gentleman was an Irishman of the old school. Jumping to his feet at the close of the recital, he shouted, 'Ladies and gintlemin: I move thray cheers for Mr. Lott's speech.'

"The cheers were vociferously given.

"After the oration of the day, the crowd adjourned to the barbecue.

"In the course of the afternoon a skirmish occurred between the Americans and a crowd of 'Sydney Ducks' (emigrants from Australia). The latter persisted in cheering for Queen Victoria. Some sneering remark about President Fillmore excited resentment, and the 'Sydney Ducks,' after a hard fought battle, were forced to recognize the supremacy of the American Eagle. The day ended with a glorious drunk, participated in generally by the public."

The thriving orchard community of Paradise is an example of how times change. This place obtained its name from a saloon there in the Fifties called Pair O' Dice, which in later days by "corruption" became Paradise.

Coal from Coal Canyon, near Oroville, was mined in the first half of the Sixties. Experiments were conducted in manufacturing gas from the coal, but the attempts were not successful.

Captain Yuba, Stringtown's Chief

One of the most notable figures of the early period was Yuba, chieftain of an Indian tribe, and generally referred to by the whites as Captain Yuba.

Captain Yuba was in appearance and character the type of Indian immortalized by Fenimore Cooper. He was fully six feet tall, straight as an arrow, brave to the point of rashness, and of keen and superior intelligence.

When the whites first appeared in search of gold, Captain Yuba gave way for about three years to his acquired appetite for firewater.

At the end of that time he announced that he had received a revelation in which the Great Spirit told him that he must quit drinking firewater, make the other Indians of his tribe do the same, and that the immorality of his people must be corrected or they would be wiped from the face of the earth.

Following the revelation, Captain Yuba ordered a council of the tribe to be called at their gathering place near Stringtown, a mining camp on the South Fork of the Feather River, so-called because of the manner in which the cabins of the miners were "strung out" along the stream.

At this conference Captain Yuba, with the greatest solemnity and in the most impressive manner, told his tribesmen of the revelation that he had received and pictured to them the fate of the tribe if its warning was not heeded.

Captain Yuba's efforts to reform his tribe failed, but he battled to the end against the vices of the white man, that they were acquiring.

Previous to the advent of the whites it was the custom of the tribe to send an army of warriors every four or five years to the Nevada salt beds after salt. The warriors were accompanied by squaws, who acted as carriers. To reach the salt it was necessary for the Indians to fight their way through territory occupied by enemy tribes. These trips generally occupied a part of two seasons. Sometimes the party never returned.

Captain Yuba, while sub-chief of the tribe, commanded two or three of these expeditions, and on each occasion, he and his party returned with the salt.

The fact that Captain Yuba's features were those of a white man, although his hair and complexion were those of an Indian, and the further fact that there appeared to be in the tribe to which he belonged something of a royal family, led the miners to believe that in some unaccountable manner, white blood flowed in Captain Yuba's veins.

This view was strengthened at a later time by the discovery in the same neighborhood as that the tribe had occupied of a most peculiar and unusual document.

Sometime during the year 1879, two miners desiring to build a cabin, cut down an oak tree. On its outside the tree appeared to be solid, but on being cut into, it proved to be hollow, the bark having grown around and enclosed a cavity in the tree. In this cavity a roll of manuscript was found It was wrapped in such a manner that the writing was still legible.

This manuscript, upon translation, purported to have been written by two men who had strayed from Cortez' army in Mexico in 1559, had worked their way north to the point where the manuscript was found, and there, lost in a wilderness and fearing death, had placed the record of their wanderings in a tree in the thought and with the hope that some day it might be found.

After the discovery of this manuscript, the theory was generally accepted that one or both of these men had cast their lot with an Indian tribe, and that they, by reason of their superior intelligence, had become the rulers of the tribe; that from them sprang the royal family, the last member of which was Captain Yuba.

That Captain Yuba's fears for the safety of his tribe were well founded, is evidenced by an article in an Oroville newspaper of July, 1865. The article reads:

"On Saturday and Sunday last, the Indians composing the tribe known as the Stringtown Indians assembled at the old Indian graveyard on Oregon Creek, near Stringtown, and held a 'grand cry' meeting. There were two hundred present. It was a general feast and cry. The eatables prepared for the occasion were about one ton of flour baked into flapjacks, and several barrels of acorn soup. This was indulged in freely by the red skins, and all white visitors present were generously invited to participate. The past year has been a great time of mortality in this tribe. Indicative of this, every squaw wore the usual badge of mourning, a tarred face. For two days and nights the woods surrounding were made hideous with the Indian distress cry. This tribe was once considered the most powerful on the Yuba and Feather Rivers, but now numbers in all not over two hundred. Last week three of this number died. They are fast passing away. A few years, and none of this tribe will exist."

When Hunting Grizzlies Was Every-day Sport

In 1843 General John Bidwell made his first trip into the upper Sacramento Valley. He was searching for stolen horses.

He tells of one of his experiences as follows: "Approaching Butte Creek we had an encounter with grizzly bears. In the spring of the year these bears lived principally on the plains, and especially in the little depressions in the plains. The first of the band we saw made for the timber, two or three miles distant; soon another came into sight, and another, and still more. At one time there were sixteen in the drove. Of course we chased them, but had no desire to overtake them. I pursued one of the largest alone. He was the largest grizzly I had ever seen, and I had the keenest desire to shoot him. I rode almost onto him, but every time I raised my gun, my horse began bucking. My desire to shoot the bear became so great that I charged as near as I dared and dismounted, intending to get a shot and mount before he could get me. But the moment I was on the ground, it was all that I could do to hold my horse, which jumped and plunged and sawed my hands with the rope. When I could look at the bear, I found that he had stopped, reared and was looking toward me and the horse. My hair, I think, stood straight up and I was delighted when the bear turned and ran from me.

"The next morning we were early in the saddle and on our way, and in a few miles ride took further lessons in the pastime of chasing grizzly bears. I pursued a large one and a very swift one. When following a grizzly you must run by the side and not immediately behind him, for he can more easily catch you if you do. I was chasing too directly behind him, and before I could turn, so close was I that when the grizzly turned and struck, his claws touched the tail of my horse, and for a hundred yards at every jump he struck my horse's tail. Coming to better ground, we soon left the bear, and as soon as he turned, I turned after him. I heard him plunge into a stream and swim across it. Stationing myself where I could see him as he came out, I shot as he stood on his hind feet. The blood spurted out of his nostrils two or three feet high, and he bounded about one hundred yards and died. These scenes were common, of daily and almost hourly occurrence."

Before the Gold Hunters Came

Before the discovery of gold at Bidwell Bar on the Feather River, in 1848, the area now comprising Butte County and known in the gold days as the Feather River diggings, was largely an unknown and an unexplored land. Its mountains were unmapped and its rivers unnamed. Its fertile plains were the home of thousands of elk, deer, antelope and wild horses. In the mountains great grizzly bears roamed, making occasional forays into the valley. The primitive redman reigned supreme, except for a few places where grants had been made by the Mexican government. Along the banks of the river and creeks, and in the mountain valleys, hundreds of Indian villages were to be found.

Of the change that a few years wrought, General Bidwell wrote:

"It is not easy to conceive and understand the change in the condition of the country. We seldom or never were out of sight of game, deer, elk, antelope and grizzly bear. The snow-capped mountains on each side of the valley, seen through the clear atmosphere of spring, the plains brilliant with flowers, the luxuriant herbage, all truly combined to lend enchantment to the view. In fact, the valley with two or three unimportant exceptions, was as new as when Columbus discovered America."

The Forties marked the beginning of the occupation of the upper Sacramento Valley. By the middle of that decade a number of land grants had been made in the Butte County area. However, by 1847, the white population of the entire Sacramento Valley, according to a report made to General Sutter, numbered but 289 persons.

A glimpse of life upon one of these Mexican grants in Butte County is given by Peter J. Burnett, a member of the first party of Oregon emigrants and later California's first governor. In his reminiscences he writes: "In passing down the valley, we encamped one evening near the house of an old settler named Potter. He lived in a very primitive manner. His yard in front of his adobe building, was full of chips of fresh beef hung upon the lines to dry. He had been to the mines, had employed Indians to work for him, and had grown rich."

Cattle raising was the sole business of these grant holders and their successors. The Spanish cattle, distinguished by their long horns and small bodies, roamed the plains. They were valuable only for their hides and tallow, which were shipped on flat bottomed boats down the river to trading posts.

Agriculture as it is now practiced was unknown on the grants. The raising of cattle and horses was practically the sole business of the early grant holders.

The Indians belonged to the Maidu, or Maideh nation. Although they lived as peacefully together as an Indian tribe, they were careful to place their camps or villages so as to prevent surprise. To obtain water they had to live near a stream or spring. In the mountains they generally selected a sheltered open cove, where an enemy could not easily approach within a bow shot without being discovered, and where there was a knoll in the cover that would assure drainage. But there were frequently hill stations or outposts, commanding a still wider prospect, in which either the warriors alone or the whole village would take their residence when the war was raging. These were generally on bold promontories, overlooking a stream; but there are indications that they contained substantial lodges, and even the dance house or council chamber wherein the warriors would assemble for deliberation and perhaps for council.

The Maidu Indians had a number of distinctive dances, each celebrated in its yearly season. The Holulupai Maidu (located near the present site of Oroville) celebrated the Acorn (literally the All-Eating Dance) in the Autumn soon after the winter rains

The haunts of the Indian and the gold diggers have now become a favorite resort of motion picture companies. The magnificent scenery of the Feather River Canyon has furnished the setting for a number of notable plays. The above picture is that of Anita Stewart and was taken in the Feather River Canyon near Belden, where her company was then engaged in producing a photoplay.

set in, to assure a bountiful crop of acorns for the following year.

Assembling together throughout their villages, they danced together in two circles, the men in one circle, the women in the other. The former decorated themselves with feathers, the latter with beads. After a certain length of time the dance ceased and two venerable priests came forward with gorgeous head-dresses and long mantles of black eagle's feathers. Each in turn made a long and earnest application to the spirits, chanting short sentences in their occult, priestly language. At long intervals the listening Indians responded "Ho!", the equivalent of our Amen.

The dance was resumed, time being kept by one Indian stamping with his foot on a large, hollow slab. The exercises would continue for many hours. At intervals acorn porridge was handed out.

The Clover Dance was celebrated in the blossom time of clover. Upon the ripening of manzanita berries came the Manzanita Dance. The Great Spirit Dance was held in propitiation of demons.

The Dance of the Dead or the Weeping Dance, came about the end of August. The Indians brought together large quantities of baskets and food and other things they believed that their dead required in the other world. Everything was made new for the occasion. The dance was held near the graves of the dead. The Indians seated themselves on the graves, men and squaws together, and as twilight closed in upon them, began a mournful, wailing cry and ululation for the dead of the year.

After a time they arose and, forming a circle about a central fire, commenced a dance, accompanied by the hoarse and deathly rattle of the Indian chant. The dancing and the singing went on for hours. From time to time the gifts brought to the dead were thrown into the flames. All through the night the funeral dance went on without cessation. The chanting became wilder and more frantic. Faster and faster the offerings were cast into the flames. Now some squaw, if not restrained, would fling herself headlong into the burning mass. As daybreak approached, with one frantic rush, they seized the remainder of the gifts and hurled them into the fire lest dawn should come before the year-long hunger of the ghosts was appeased.

General Bidwell describes Indian life as he saw it in 1847, as follows: "The Indians were almost as wild as deer and wholly unclad, save that the women wore a skirt-like covering divided at the sides, made of tule, a kind of rush, which was fastened to a belt. When I began a survey, not having enough white men, I had to use Indians. In clearing away brush and brambles it soon became necessary to furnish something in the way of clothing, including shoes, pantaloons, and shirts, which were often removed by them as soon as the work was done, and carried home to their village to be brought back in the morning and worn while at work. They soon learned to wear their clothes day and night, until worn out."

In the early period the bow and arrow were the weapons used by the Indians. To poison the arrow points, the liver of a deer was secured, then put where rattlesnakes could bite it, afterwards left to partially decay and then dried rapidly. The arrow points were moistened and then passed through the dried mass a number of times. A wound from such an arrow generally caused instantaneous death.

In the manufacture of arrow points, jasper and flint were principally used. One source of supply from which the warriors of the Feather River District obtained their flint was a cave in Table Mountain, across the Feather River from the present site of Oroville. We quote a short item that appeared in a bulletin of the American Museum of Natural History, bearing on this subject:

"Near Oroville was one of the best known spots for getting flint from a cave in or near Table Mountain. The opening to the cave was very small, but once in, the size was such, that a man could stand upright. A person going to get flint must crawl in, and then throw ahead of him beads or dried meat as offerings to the spirits for the flint he was about to take. One was allowed to take only so much flint as he could break off at a single blow. The flint obtained, the person had to crawl out backwards. If the regulations were not complied with, the person would have bad luck, the flint would not chip well, or would fail to kill."

RIDING THE HURRICANE DECK OF A MULE

Not only were there freight trains of mules, but there were passenger trains as well, and the hurricane deck of a mule was a customary mode of travel in the Fifties. Some of the drivers of these mule trains were famous characters, and the skill with which they could load freight onto a mule was little short of phenomenal. The trained pack mule learned to assist in this packing process by bracing himself. The public learned to have a high respect for the intelligence of the mule, and asserted that that animal would attempt any trail until he smelled an Indian track or a bear track, when it was almost impossible to drive him farther.

It was in the latter part of the Fifties that the first buggy was brought into Buttte County.

Statue to James Marshall, who first discovered gold in California.
This statue was erected at Coloma where Marshall
made his momentous discovery

Building of the Western Pacific

Back of the construction of a railroad through the Feather River Canyon is the story of over half a century of hope, ambition and effort. The Western Pacific is the realization of a dream that the pioneers first dreamed and that decade after decade they and those who followed them attempted to transmute into actuality.

When the Central Pacific was first projected, the advantages of the Feather River Canyon over the higher Truckee route were strongly urged by delegations of citizens from Butte and Plumas Counties. But the settlements along the Truckee route were larger and more numerous, and considerations of local traffic predominated in the final determination of the location of the railroad.

The failure, however, of the proponents of the Feather River to secure the adoption of their route by the Central Pacific did not abate their interest in nor efforts to secure a railroad through the Feather's wonderful gorge.

In 1867 these efforts took what was believed to be tangible form in the incorporation of the Oroville and Virginia City Railroad. The purpose of the company as set forth in the articles of incorporation was to construct a railroad between Oroville, California, and Virginia City, Nevada, via Beckwourth Pass, following approximately the same route as the Western Pacific now follows. The legality of the incorporation was attacked and in 1871 the Supreme Court declared it unconstitutional.

This decision gives an interesting sidelight on methods of financing of the period. The subscription to the stock of the road aggregated $110,000. The law required that ten per cent of the stock subscription must be actually paid up prior to incorporation. The evidence revealed that instead of $11,000 being paid into the treasury, but $100 cash had actually been paid. The balance of $10,900 was paid by the promoters of the road drawing a check payable to themselves in that amount on a bank in which they had no funds. The check was never presented for payment, but the technicalities necessary for incorporation had apparently been met. One mile of the road was actually graded out of Oroville.

In 1873 the effort to secure a railroad through the Feather River Canyon was renewed. This time a narrow gauge road was proposed. The road named Reno and Oroville as terminals. Nothing came of the plan.

The Eighties witnessed a number of surveys and reconnaissances of the Feather River Canyon for railroad purposes. In 1881 the Sierra Iron Company, which had extensive iron deposits near the present station of

Along the Western Pacific in the Feather River Canyon

To the builders of the highways
That skirt the Canyon's brink,
To the men who bind the roadbed fast,
To the men who grade and the men who blast,
I raise my glass and drink.

Theirs the great endeavor,
And the deed of high emprize,
For they fight with naked hands
'Gainst forest, swamp and shifting sands,
And the fury of the skies.

To the builders who have fallen,
Whose graves mark out the line,
To the blind, who never more shall see,
To the maimed and halt in their misery,
In silence drink your wine.

For them no crashing volleys,
Nor roll of muffled drums,
Only the roar of the great rock blast
Is their requiem song when the day is passed,
And the final darkness comes.

To the engineers, the wizards,
Whose words brook no delay;
Hearing, the sleeping glens awake,
The snow plumed hills obeisance make—
And lo! the Open Way!

For them no flaunting banners
When a bitter fight is won;
No cheering thousands in the streets,
These gallant heroes ever meet,
Though dauntless deeds be done.

—Evelyn Gunn.

Blairsden, declared its intention to build a narrow gauge line to Oroville on the west, and Reno on the east. In 1888 a reconnaissance of the canyon was made by Salt Lake capitalists to determine the possibilities that it offered for railroad construction. In

1889 the Union Pacific began a survey of the Middle Fork of the Feather River. This was concluded in 1892, but the heavy construction of the Bald Rock Canyon prevented the adoption of the route.

Between 1890 and 1900 there were the usual number of schemes for the utilization of the Feather River Canyon for railroad purposes. These were widely heralded in the press. The one event, however, of permanent importance, was the reconnaissance of the Canyon by E. J. Yard, of the so-called Gould system. The trip was made incognito, and as a result was unnoticed in the press.

In 1892 a survey of the canyon was started by engineers of the San Francisco and Great Salt Lake Railroad. Within a few months after crews were placed in the field, the collapse of that railroad was announced. In 1899 an electric line was proposed, but without results.

These decades of efforts fruited in the period between 1900 and 1910 in the Western Pacific.

The story of its construction reads like a chapter from fiction.

For years it had been the ambition of the Gould people to extend their lines into California. The reconnaissance made by E. J. Yard in the early nineties had convinced him that the Feather River Canyon offered the most feasible route into the State.

In 1902 it was decided that the time had come to strike from Salt Lake across Nevada to California. The Denver and Rio Grande enjoyed a large freight traffic interchanged with the Harriman lines at Ogden, Utah. It was the desire of the Gould interests to retain this traffic while the preliminary work upon the new road was under way. Accordingly every movement was veiled with the greatest secrecy.

A large part of the Feather River section was located as mineral and timber claims. It was planned that after these locations had been made, the announcement would follow that a railroad was necessary to market the timber and to take in supplies for mines and mills. Under this cloak surveying crews were put in the field, and the work of locating the railroad started.

It soon became evident that men experienced in railroad location and railroad surveys were needed. Experienced engineers were sent to California under assumed names and the work was taken over from the local engineers who were previously in charge.

About the time that the work of locating the timber and mining claims started, the Stockton and Beckwourth Pass Railroad appeared on the scene.

(Continued on Page 34)

Mt. Lassen Where the North Fork Heads

Situated at the headwaters of the North Fork of the Feather River is Mt. Lassen, famous now as the Nation's only active volcano, and known in the early days of California's history as one of the pilot peaks by which early explorers and pathfinders located themselves.

Lassen's eruption in recent times began on Decoration Day, May 30th, 1914.

For nearly a year succeeding eruptions occurred frequently, culminating in the great outbreak of May 19th and 20th, and May 22nd, 1915, which probably closed the last chapter in the geological history of this volcano.

Geologists place the period of greatest volcanic activity in the Lassen region as occurring probably 2,000,000 years ago.

Up to the 1915 eruption, Cinder Cone was believed to be the most recent expression of volcanic activity.

Among the notable features of this volcanic park are Chaos Crags, which rise to an altitude of 9000 feet above the sea level and 3000 feet above the ancient lavas which form the base. The devastated area of the 1915 eruption in the head of Hat and Lost Creeks, is perhaps the most awe-inspiring spectacle of the park. Here the mountain was rent asunder by the force of the eruption.

Canyons have scoured deeply into the ancient lavas of Broke-Off Mountain in the southeast portion of the park.

View of Mt. Lassen in Eruption

Geyser areas are found in the park, which are declared second only in interest to the Yellowstone geysers.

Lake Tartarus, or "Boiling Lake," is one of the unique spectacles associated with the latent phases of volcanic activity. In the same region is the Devil's Kitchen, where an angler may catch a trout in one stream and, without changing his position, throw it into boiling water and thus cook his fish.

Bumpass' Hell, two miles south of the peak, is a miniature inferno of unique interest.

The park is to be developed with scenic auto roads and trails, but otherwise this wonderland will be kept for all time just as God made and intended it to be.

BUILDING THE WESTERN PACIFIC RAILROAD—*Continued*

(Continued from Page 33)

A group of San Francisco capitalists were back of this project. They took their plan back to New York and the first office they entered there was that of the Goulds. In order to control the Feather River situation, the Gould officials in New York decided to tie up with the promoters of the Stockton and Beckwourth Pass road.

Accordingly, the Feather River Canyon was soon full of surveyors. Neither side knew that they were both working for the same people. So fearful were the Stockton and Beckwourth Pass people that something might leak out as to who was backing them, that they forbade their engineers even to speak to the road engineers or their crews. Adding zest to the engineers' war was the fact that there was wide difference of opinion between the rival camps as to the side of the river to be chosen.

Other passes were also studied. But when the survey revealed that a one per cent grade was possible by way of the Beckwourth Pass and the North Fork of the Feather River, a decision favoring it was immediately made. Financing was arranged in New York. The Gould interests revealed their hand, and bids for the construction of a new railroad into California were asked.

The contract for the construction of the railroad between Oroville and Salt

A View of the Western Pacific in the Feather River Canyon

Lake was let to the Utah Construction Company. The bid was $22,000,000 for building and grading the railroad, including a wagon road over which to move their steam shovels, etc., to the place that it was ready to lay rails. The rails were laid and depots and terminals built by the Western Pacific itself.

Construction started in Oroville in 1905. The road was approximately five years in the building. The mileage costs for grading ran from $3500 a mile for places on the desert, to as high as $100,000 a mile in the Feather River Canyon. At one time 6200 men were at work building the road in the Feather River Canyon alone, not counting the engineering crews maintained and employed by the Western Pacific. The most difficult work encountered was the construction of the Spring Garden Tunnel. An underground stream was encountered and for five months workmen battled with this stream. As fast as workmen took out material, the stream would carry it in again. During the five months' battle, the tunnel did not advance one foot. At the end of the five months, the stream had been conquered and the work of driving the tunnel was continued.

Considering the magnitude of the task, the number of fatalities was not large, but at that over one hundred men lost their lives in constructing the road. Few people realize as they view the magnificent scenery of the Feather River Canyon from a Pullman window, the cost of the road in money and in men, the skill in engineering that it required, and the dreams of decades of which it became the realization.

Commandments to California Wives

Entered according to Act of Congress in the year 1855, by James M. Hutchings in the Clerk's office of the U. S. District Court for California.

Now it came to pass that as thy servant sat alone and at night watching the dying embers of his cabin fire, behold the latch of his cabin door was lifted and before him stood an angel clothed in female attire. As in duty-bound I immediately arose from my only stool, and invited her to be seated; this she gracefully declined; but placing her white and beautiful fingers upon the bosom of my woolen shirt, in a voice of musical distinctness, she thus addressed me: "Young man, hast thou courage?" I was almost speechless, for I felt what little I possessed fast oozing away, and I modestly answered that I had none to boast of, yet "dare do all that may become a man." "It is enough," she replied. "I therefore commission thee to give the following—

Commandments to California Wives:

I.

Thou shalt not "put on airs" of self-importance, nor indulge in day dreams of extravagance, nor allow thy vanity and love of dress to turn thy head, and unfit thee for the sober duties of life, or make thee merely an expensive toy and walking advertisement of the latest fashions.

II.

Thou shalt not believe thyself to be an angel—all but the wings—nor over-estimate thine own and under-estimate thy husband's value; because the scarcity of thy sex leads men to bow, almost in worship, to silk or calico made into woman's garments; neither shalt thou be intoxicated by the personal attractions and flattering attentions of men with finger-rings, fine apparel and prancing horses; nor by the glittering equipage and wonderful promises of the unprincipled and gay gallant, lest thy weakness and folly tempt thee to prefer him to thy husband, and soon under the plea of "incompatibility of temperament" or other phantom of the imagination—thou become dissatisfied and in the end "seek a separation," or "pray for a divorce," to gratify thy vain desires or cover thy sin.

III.

Thou shalt not consider it fashionable, cleanly nor economical to sweep the streets with one hundred dollar dresses—when at home thou considered thyself fortunate to get calico—nor to promenade muddy sidewalks in long satin robes and bedraggled underclothes; nor to wear jewels and flowers on thy head while thy feet go "flippety-clock" in buskin shoes run down at the heel, and discover to strangers the holes in thy stockings.

IV.

Thou shalt not starve thyself and thy family twenty-nine days out of thirty to feast thy circle and give a party; nor by the purchase of expensive gew-gaws and finery keep thy husband poor; nor run up bills for frills and furbelows while the dry goods merchant and thy husband are at their wits' end how to pay their way; nor lose a half day shopping to invest four bits. Neither shalt thou devour all thy savings at cotillion parties and balls; nor waste thy substance by improvidence nor neglect.

V.

Thou shalt not fret nor sulk nor faint nor fly into hysterics because thine unfortunate husband cannot buy for thee "that beautiful moon made of such nice green cheese," and a riding dress to match; nor quit his business at any moment and take you out riding to—Paradise. Neither shalt thou ride or walk with other men nor associate with profligates and spendthrifts in the ball room or by the wayside in preference to thy husband; nor, under the excuse of saving his purse, treat him as a simpleton or a slave, to stay at home and nurse the children, or follow thee—at a proper distance—to await thy pleasure or carry thy lap dog.

VI.

Thou shalt not accept presents of Cashmere shawls, specimen shawl pins, embroidered elastics, diamond rings or other baubles as the price of thy husband's and thine own dishonor—supposing they will bring thee happiness;—for—after thou hast forsaken honor, husband, children and home—as ministers of retribution they will dog thy footsteps and haunt thy sleep with withering memories of the happy Past and shut forever out the angel images of innocence and love that hovered about thy parents'

During the Middle Fifties a series of elaborately decorated articles moralizing on life in the gold diggings of California sprang into popularity. Above is a photograph of one of these series entitled "Commandments to California Wives." It shows the general style of the other articles, which included "Articles In A Miner's Creed," "The Miners' Ten Commandments," and other matters of a like character. These articles throw an illuminative light upon life in California at that period.

dwelling and in thy husband's home—while thy poor abandoned children, the objects of charity and pity, wander as outcasts and he, that was thy husband, perish in sorrow and the gutter—a miserable drunkard or a broken-hearted, premature old man.

VII.

Thou shalt not substitute sour looks for pickles; nor a fiery temper for stove wood; nor cross words for kindlings; nor trifling talk for light bread; nor tart language for dessert. Neither shalt thou serve up cold looks or cold meals for breakfast, nor scoldings and hard potatoes for dinner, nor what remains of the other two meals for supper—no, not even on washing days. Neither shalt thou allow hard feelings and unwashed dishes to accumulate, nor withhold either secrets or shirt buttons from the bosom of thy husband; and never omit little kindnesses of any kind.

VIII.

Thou shalt not neglect to make thy person and thy home attractive—that when thy husband comes from his daily toil, thy cheering looks of loving welcome may greet his footsteps and charm him into forgetfulness of all but thee. And should he be unfortunate, as many are, thou shalt not increase his sorrow as many do by weeping and repining, but with all thy noblest sympathy and womanly love, seek to lift the heavy burden from his manly heart; and, thus renewed, again to dare the rugged and slippery steep that leads to fortune and success—believing "there is no such word as fail" while thou art near to cheer him on and share with him the victory.

IX.

Thou shalt not seek to break up friendships and injure character by fabricating slander. Neither shalt thou indulge in insinuating innuendos; nor use half spoken and surmising sentences, nor suspicious and knowing or upturned looks. Neither shalt thou go about with thy gadding-needle, gossip-thread and scandal-basket of evil speaking with which to mend the character and manners of thy neighbors; for when thy handiwork is returned unto thee—as it will be—magnified, twisted and changed, thou wilt reply in anger, "I never said it," yet will not be believed, but henceforth be considered a busy-body and a mischief maker.

X.

Thou shalt not give these commandments a revengeful interpretation; nor curl thy lip in insulted contempt. Neither shalt thou take pleasure in thinking "Won't these suit Mrs. So-and-So!" but examine carefully where they speak unto thee, that peradventure by their admonition and by reading twice a week the last chapter of Ephesians, thou mayest profit thereby.

LASTLY!

To Unmarried Ladies:—Thou shalt not become weary of waiting for thy lover's return; nor expect him at thy side before his purse is full; nor forsake him because he is poor; nor marry another because he is rich (for here the rich become poor and the poor become rich). Neither shalt thou hesitate—if thou lovest him—when he sendeth for thee; yet let her remain who if a room is not carpeted or a dinner needs cooking, or a shirt requires washing, expects to drown irrevocably in briny tears or die immediately in agonizing spasms because she "never soiled her fingers before and now —it is so provoking"—poor thing! Moreover whisper ye to the wives at home that they "cut up no capers" while, uncheered and alone—frequently against hope—their husbands toil unremittingly on from month to month without one murmuring thought of what they suffer or forego for the dear ones, far, far away. Amen. So mote it be.

FORTY-NINE.

A case of record in the justice's court at Thompson Flat, a mining camp across the river from Oroville, relates that two citizens of that place being brought into court for some infraction of the law following an escapade in which they had become involved were fined "champagne for the town."

Diamonds in the gravel washings at Cherokee were first found in 1864. The diamonds were sent East and cut and were pronounced stones of the first water.

INDIAN TROUBLES OF THE EARLY DAYS—*Continued*

(Continued from Page 18)

bushes and began to hurl boulders and rocks upon the dead body of the little boy.

Six other Indians then joined them. One of these latter Indians had one large foot and one small foot. It was none other than the dreaded "Big Foot."

The Indians seized the two other children and started for the mountains. They traveled until late that night up the steep mountain sides, through the brush and over the rough rocks. That night they camped in the bed of a dry stream.

In the morning the boy, John, was taken out, beaten with clubs and stoned to death.

The march was then taken up again. The Indians told the little girl, Thankful, that when they reached their campoodie they would tie her to a post, put wood around her and burn her to death. They pictured the Indians dancing about the pyre. And to show the torture they would inflict upon her, they repeatedly stuck her with sharp sticks.

Thus they traveled hour after hour. Finally the girl was left with one of the Indians while his companions went ahead a short distance, apparently to reconnoiter. He desired to join them. She asked that she be allowed to rest for a moment upon a prominent rock while he went ahead. If she were only allowed a short rest, she assured him that she would be able to travel with them without further delay. Her guard finally consented to the plan, threatening, however, to kill her if she stirred from the rock.

Time after time he looked back, but the little girl was always sitting where she had been left. Apparently convinced that she would not attempt to escape, the Indian disappeared for a moment. Quick as a flash, Thankful rolled over and over from the rock into the ravine. The girl ran at breakneck speed for a mile or so, and finally hid in a creek bank under a pile of driftwood.

The Indians apparently soon took up the search. At one time they passed within a few feet of her hiding place. Apparently fearing pursuit by the whites when the disappearance of the Lewis children was discovered and the dead body of the little boy found, they finally abandoned the search. After lying in her hiding place for hours, the little girl emerged and made her way back toward the white settlements. She at last found safety in the home of a mountain rancher.

In the meantime, the failure of the children to return home had started a searching party out for them. The body of the baby brother was found in the creek. A hue and cry went up, and scores joined in the posse organized to find and punish the Indians.

No hope was entertained that either of the other two children was alive. Word, however, soon reached the men that Thankful had escaped. With her aid the posse took up the trail of the Indians. She led them to the spot where her brother had been killed and his body was found there. The Indians themselves, however, had escaped into the almost impenetrable fastness of the rugged Deer Creek Canyon.

This and the murder of other children and the massacre of some white families, led to a war upon the Mill Creek Indians in which the tribe was almost entirely wiped out, and to the enforced deportation of other Indians to an Indian reservation near the Coast.

In 1907 workmen constructing a dam for a reservoir near Pentz, found in an old prospect hole the skeleton of a little girl. This discovery solved a tragedy of the very early Fifties. Near Pentz was a miner with two daughters, Jessie and Mary Smith. He left them one morning in his cabin while he went to work his claim. When he returned the girls were gone. The track of moccasined feet and the evidence of a struggle showed that the girls had been captured by Indians.

In a few days the older of the two, Jessie, returned. She stated that she had escaped from the Indians, and asked for her sister. She was told that despite the fact that miners for miles had joined in the search for the girls, her sister had not been found.

Jessie then told that after the Indians had seized her sister and herself, their captors had formed into two parties and the girls had been separated. That was the last that she had seen of her sister.

The identity of the skeleton found in the old prospect hole as that of Mary Smith was established by old-fashioned buttons also found there, and by long tresses of auburn hair that had made the girl noted all around the countryside. Some strands of the hair still remained.

The little girl had evidently been killed shortly after her capture and the body thrown into the old prospect hole, where it had been covered with rocks and brush.

ISHI THE ABORIGINE—*Continued*

(Continued from Page 18)

through the use of scores of Indian dialects. His efforts failed, and he frankly admitted that a true aborigine had been found in the midst of a twentieth century civilization.

When almost ready to abandon his efforts to establish a community of language, Professor Waterman used one word in the almost forgotten dialect of the North Yana Indians. The Indian recognized this, and interpreted it by signs. This led to the establishment of his tribal identity. It was finally ascertained that he was a member of the South Yana tribe, which was related to the North Yanas. In an authorized interview given to the Oroville Daily Register, Professor Waterman declared that the civilization of the Indian was of a period 20,000 years earlier than that in which he was living.

For want of a better name, Professor Waterman christened the Indian "Ishi," which means "The Man."

Ishi was taken to the Affiliated Colleges of the University of California in San Francisco. The newspapers devoted pages to him and his prowess with the bow and arrow. He was a veritable treasure house of information concerning the beliefs and practices of the South Yana Indians. He confirmed the story told by signs at Oroville of the fact that he and his companions were the remnant of the tribe and that his two companions had been killed.

Ignorant of the value of money at first, Ishi soon learned that it had a use. Thousands of people visited him weekly. He dressed as a white man, and this sealed his doom. When practically naked, he feared neither cold nor heat; but when warmly dressed he took cold, and after about three years at the Affiliated Colleges, he succumbed to pneumonia.

Thus passed the last of the Deer Creeks.

SPORTS OF THE PIONEERS

Chasing antelopes with dogs was a favorite sport in the Fifties. Bull-fights were also a favorite spectacle. Fights were also staged between grizzly bears and bulls. An account of one of these fights staged in Oroville in 1856, states that nearly thirty of the wildest bulls that could be found were brought in to fight a grizzly that had been captured in the mountains. The bear was chained and did not have a chance. As the bull charged the bear would rise up on its rear legs, slap the bull over the head or body and knock it down. One bull was killed and several others hurt so badly that they had to be hauled away. The bear was gored but once.

In 1862 residents of Dog Town rebelled at the name given to it by the pioneers and it was re-christened Magalia, interpreted as the Latin name for cottages.

Today's Epic of the Feather is Power

Written 24 years ago, this story of electric power on the Feather, requires only a few changes and additions, to be descriptive of today's developments. Some of the great power expansion projects the writer predicted with accurate vision, are just now being pressed forward by Pacific Gas and Electric Company. The banks of the Feather again teem with construction crews and tunnel men. The facts are published here as a postscript to the original story—The Editor.

On the banks of the dashing waters of the Feather River was written a goodly part of the first great epic of California—the epic of the discovery of gold, of the coming of the gold hunters, the birth of a new State, the beginning of a new West.

Today by the waters of the same stream, another great epic is being written. The story of today is not that of gold, but of a treasure greater and more valuable than gold and more beneficent in its use. Today's epic is that PERPETUAL POWER, of power available for the use of mankind as long as rain falls, snows melt and mountain streams rush to the valleys below.

Or, translated into terms of human service, the epic that the waters of the Feather tell today is that of a servant for the home who never fails; a "hired man" for the farm who never leaves; of a factory laborer who takes neither account of length of days nor hours of overtime.

Hydro-electric power has been well called the "white coal" of industry. Adapting this phase to the Feather River, that stream may be properly designated as one of the world's greatest "white coal mines."

The development of the hydro-electric industry along the Feather River illustrates how closely the past is coordinated with the present and the future.

A mining tunnel constructed at Big Bend, on the North Fork of the Feather River, first turned the attention of engineers to the possibilities that this, the main branch of the Feather River, offered for the development of hydro-electric power on the

Caribou Power Plant

largest scale west of the Mississippi River.

This tunnel had been constructed to divert the waters from the bed of the Feather River through the tunnel into Dark Creek, thus enabling the gravel of the river bed to be mined for gold.

As a mining enterprise the project was not a success. Early day miners by wingdam and sluice had mined the stream too thoroughly. As a power project, however, the tunnel, enlarged, lengthened and concreted throughout, made possible the Las Plumas power plant of the Great Western Power Company of California.

It is interesting to note that the distance by railroad from the Intake of the tunnel to the Las Plumas power plant is twelve miles. The tunnel, cutting through Big Bend, is just three and one-half miles long, and permits a total drop into the power plant of 465 feet, enabling the generation of 87,000 horsepower of electric energy.

Since the Las Plumas plant was constructed, the Great Western Power Company has completed another large power plant on the North Fork of the Feather River, approximately 50 miles above Las Plumas. This plant, known as the Caribou plant, now generates 89,000 horsepower of electric energy.

Seven other plants located at strategic points from the Caribou to a point about three miles east of Oroville are yet to be built.

These plants, using the same water over and over again, will develop the gigantic ultimate total of over 800,000 h.p.

Just how tremendous the power of this falling water in producing electric energy is, can be realized when units of electric power are translated into units of human power.

One kilowatt of electric energy is the equivalent of the power of eight men. The total power that the system of the Great Western Power Company will develop will accordingly give the power equivalent of a full day's work of an army of over 14,400,000 men.

It is of further interest to note that this power works ungrudgingly for the public at 'an average charge per kilowatt hour of approximately 1.6 cents. Again translating this into terms of human labor, for 1.6 cents the public is getting and will get the energy equivalent to the labor of a man working eight hours.

There are certain physcial facts about the Feather River that make it by general admission one of America's greatest power streams.

First in this list might be stated that the Feather River rises in a country of abundant snow fall and heavy annual precipitation. The normal annual runoff of the stream makes it the second largest of California's rivers.

A second factor is that the stream heads in one of the large valleys of the Sierra Nevadas, known from its size

View of Lake Almanor, on the headwaters of the Feather River.

since the early days of California's history as "Big Meadows." The Great Western Power Company was enabled to convert this great valley into an artificial lake by constructing a dam only 1200 feet in length and 80 feet high, at the point where the Big Meadows narrowed into the canyon. Thus the normal run-off of the Feather River in itself always very large, is augmented and controlled by the release in the summer months of waters stored during winter in Lake Almanor. At present Lake Almanor covers 15,800 acres and stores 300,000 acre feet of water. By adding 43 feet to the present height of the dam, the storage capacity of Lake Almanor can be increased to 1,250,000 acre feet. This will make it possible to impound the annual run-off of the 500 square miles of watershed that feeds the lake for a period of several years, giving absolute assurance of water even in the event of a series of successive years of low annual precipitation.

Lake Almanor today has a total capacity of 1,308,000 acre feet. Its flooded area is 28,257 acres in extent.

A third factor that has made the Feather River power development one of the outstanding features of hydroelectric power in the United States is the opportunity for the successive development of power that the long course of the river offers. The water drops a distance of over 4000 feet in the 75 miles of distance between Lake Almanor and Oroville. This fall is evenly distributed, and at the same time the contour of the canyon is such that it makes it possible for the water to be diverted a number of times by tunnel and subsequently dropped to power plants located within an economical construction distance of the place at which the water was diverted. As noted previously, the company plans the use and re-use of the same water in seven additional power plants.

A fourth factor is that as the water leaves the Feather River Canyon it debouches on the valley in a rich agricultural and horticultural section, where the demand for water for irrigation is already great and yearly growing greater. Through the Western Canal Company, the Great Western Power Company sells its waters to irrigate an immense acreage of valley and foothill land, planted to orchards and groves, to rice, alfalfa and the scores of diversified crops that the fertile lands and the favorable climate of

Las Plumas Power Plant
(Big Bend)

Butte County produce.

Thus irrigation completes the cycle. Perpetual Power is perpetuated in Perpetual Food.

The Great Western Power Company speeds its products almost instantaneously over great steel towers and miles of copper and aluminum wire over two hundred miles away to San Francisco and the cities of the San Francisco Bay by submarine cables. Substations and lateral power lines along the route complete the task of distribution in the affluent territory that the company serves.

1948 Postscript

The Great Western Power Company, foreseeing continued growth of Northern California, built a third unit of the Feather River power system in 1928 when it completed Buck's Creek powerhouse, near Storrie. Although located on the River, Buck's Creek generators are powered by the waters of the watershed that feeds Buck's Creek and Grizzly Creek reservoirs and are dropped to the turbines from an elevation 2561 feet above the powerhouse floor. This is a record "static head" in hydroelectric generation.

In 1930 the Great Western Power Company was merged into the P. G. and E. interconnected system which now serves all of Central and Northern California. P. G. and E. now is in the midst of a vast expansion program which by the end of 1951 will have added nearly 2,000,000 horsepower to its generating capacity. An important part of that program is the further development of the Feather River's hydroelectric resources.

Currently, construction crews are at work on two projects—the new Rock Creek powerhouse, capacity 169,000 horsepower and Cresta powerhouse, capacity 101,000 horsepower. The two new generating stations, with appurtenant switching and other facilities will cost a total of $61,800,000. they will bring the total Feather River power capacity to 514,000 horsepower, with four other powerhouse sites yet to be developed.

When the entire program is completed the Feather River will have reached its peak of usefulness in the generation of electricity for beneficial utilization by the committees of Northern California. And, having done their work in driving the generators of power, the waters of the Feather, their usefulness unimpaired, flow on to the valley lands for irrigation of farm lands and for domestic service in valley communities.

SPANISH MEALS IN PRE-GOLD PERIOD; MILKING A SPORT

Before the advent of the Fortyniner, the Spaniards' had a fairly standardized meal four times a day, writes Harry C. Peterson in one of his interesting articles on early life in California.

At breakfast, usually at daybreak, he had milk mixed with a little pinole of maize, very finely sifted, and well sweetened with sugar. Chocolate, with bread or biscuit and a little butter, was also part of the fare in many households.

About 9 o'clock in the morning a regular breakfast was indulged in, consisting of good fresh beef or veal, usually roasted; well-fried beans and a cup of coffee, or tea, or even milk. The bread used was sometimes made of wheaten flour, but more often of maize; circular in shape, flattened out very thin, and baked over a slow fire on a flat, earthen pan.

The Spaniard's dinner was at noon. Beef or mutton broth, well-peppered, with rice, cabbage, garbanzos and other vegetables cooked with it, served as the basis of the meal. From this was taken the soup. The vegetables combined with the beef made a separate dish, usually with various condiments to help out the appetite.

Then came the fried beans, followed by some sweetmeat.

During the middle of the afternoon wine would be served. At night a light supper of meat ragout or roast with beans, completed the day's eating.

On Friday fish was substituted for the meat.

Milk was probably the scarcest of all the articles of food on the native's table, despite the hundreds of thousands of cattle that roamed the great valleys. But the job of milking in those days was no sinecure; it was always a comedy, and often a tragedy.

It required three persons to milk a cow then; one held her head by the horns, another held the reata confining her hind legs, while the third milked with one hand, holding a tumbler, or teacup, or bean jar with the other in which to catch the milk, for milk pails were unknown to the Spaniard.

The ranchero, his wife and daughters and any visitors at the ranch derived much pleasure watching these daily milkings. In San Francisco, one of the missionaries stationed at Dolores boasted he was the only person on the peninsula who was able to sell fresh milk at Kotzebue's ship, delivering two bottles daily. The good padre considered it a great feat to have so subdued a cow that he could have her milk regularly.

The Conquest of the Middle Feather

This is the story of pioneers, not of 1849 and the Fifties, but of the present day and the present generation.

It is the discovery of a gold lake, real and actual, and neither a fantasy nor a phantom, as was the gold lake of pioneer days.

It is the story of old U-I-NO, dreaded by the Indians as the home of a destroying monster, conquered and bound; the story of Bald Rock Canyon, as the moderns know U-I-NO, explored, mapped and beaten; the story of the last unknown fastness of the Sierra Nevadas conquered and exploited and made accessible to all.

The story of the conquest of the Middle Fork of the Feather River is the story of a battle that began with the pioneer miners who at the cost of many lives, tried in vain to pass the portals of Bald Rock Canyon in search of the gold holes that they felt would be found there.

Everywhere else the tide of the invading gold hunters swept on unchecked. But as the miners passed Bidwell Bar, on the Middle Fork, they were stopped at the west portal of Bald Rock Canyon. And as they swept down from the sources of the Middle Fork, on the East Sierras, the tide stopped at the east portal of Bald Rock Canyon.

That four-mile stretch remained a mystery and a secret. The Indians avoided it as a place possessed of the evil one. There is no record that either Indians or white men ever traversed it until 1907, when two engineers of the U. S. Geological Survey arrived in Oroville, stating that after a trip filled with hairbreadth escapes they had made their way from the east to the west end of this canyon.

The reason for the continued failure of attempts at the exploration of that stretch of the Middle Fork that is generally known as Bald Rock Canyon, is to be found in the formation.

Bald Rock itself, or as it should be called, U-I-NO, rises a sheer 3000 feet above the bed of the river. On the other side of the river is also towering granite. The formation is identical with that of the Yosemite Valley with the exception that on the Middle Feather there is no broad valley between the cliffs, but they dip into a V-shaped trough through which the Middle Feather rushes and tumbles over rapids and cascades, through whirlpools and deep and treacherous gorges. Boulders of enormous size that can be scaled only with ladders, block the course of the stream.

It was this four-mile canyon, comparable only to the Yosemite Valley in its awe-inspiring grandeur, that made the Middle Feather the one river

A Glimpse Into the Canyon of the Middle Feather

of California unknown and unexplored, unsurveyed and unmapped. The Middle Feather is the shortest route from Nevada into Central California. But railroad engineers who came to study its possibilities turned back, foiled at the task that confronted them.

The story of the conquest of the Middle Feather is the story of Power. What Gold could not achieve, Power made possible.

In the very early years of the present century, when attention first was directed to the possibilities of the development of hydro-electric power along the streams of the Northern Sierras, William Watson, an engineer

of Quincy, turned to the Middle Feather as a feasible supply of power for Oroville. He invaded Bald Rock Canyon farther than anyone previously had gone, and acquired a more complete knowledge of that section of the Middle Feather than anyone else had. There his project stopped.

In 1907 engineers of the U. S. Geological Survey traversed the bed of the canyon and gave added information concerning this heretofore unknown region.

As interest in the development of hydro-electric power progressed, engineers again turned their eyes to the Middle Feather.

In San Francisco a group of men had

developed what was known as the Constant Angle Arch Dam, a dam that had attracted the attention of both the engineering and financial world by reason of the strength of the structures and the cheapness of the construction, as demonstrated by their very recently completed power project at Bullard's Bar on the North Fork of the Yuba River, which is Feather River's nearest neighbor on the south.

The officials and engineers of this company saw in the Middle Feather the possibility of developing one of the premier power stations of the West.

On its upper reaches the river was comparatively level, flowing through broad valleys that offered opportunity for the economical storage of water.

It was fed by mountain lakes that drew their water from the heaviest snow area of the entire Sierra range.

The big power fall of the river was confined to a relatively short distance, thus making possible economical unit costs in developing power.

And so the Constant Angle Arch Dam Company some six years ago began quietly acquiring the water and power rights by the purchase of sites and filing upon the waters of the Middle Feather and the lakes and streams that fed it.

William Watson, whose knowledge of Bald Rock Canyon was the most complete of any engineer, was placed in the field to make surveys and further study the river and Bald Rock Canyon, surveys and studies that he had started twenty years before.

The battle against Bald Rock was again on, this time not for the gold that it was thought it might contain, but for the power that it was known its waters did contain. This time engineers, experienced in their profession particularly in this line of endeavor and matured by reason of having constructed like projects in similarly difficult situations, had carefully planned the campaign.

Instead of a frontal attack against the gates of the canyon, the engineers adopted a new strategy, and the canyon was subjected to flank attacks. From place to place along the ridge of the canyon, trails were projected as far down the cliffs as they could be built, and then with ropes and ladders and chains, the men were lowered to the places below where it was necessary that lines be run. Piece by piece the area was thus surveyed and mapped.

Four years spent in this work revealed conclusively that the judgment of the officials and engineers of the Constant Angle Arch Dam Company that the Middle Feather could be made one of the premier power streams of the West was correct.

The Feather River Power Company was organized to carry on this work

and the financing program assured. The first unit calls for an outlay of more than $12,000,000, which has already commenced being spent in the conquest of the river.

Plans for the development of power through successive plants were formed and specifications for tunnels and power houses drawn. They were submitted to the Federal and State authorities having legal jurisdiction over them and were approved in every respect.

There are to be six of these plants in all. They will develop more than 200,000 horse power of electric energy in a dry year. In Bald Rock Canyon itself five miles of tunnel will be driven, and the water will be dropped more than 1000 feet through steel pipes to a power house near Bean Creek.

To feed these plants, in addition to the normal flow of the Middle Feather, over 300,000 acre feet of stream water yearly now going unused to the ocean will be stored. After completing its duty in developing power, this water will be utilized below Oroville for much needed irrigation.

This storage will be sufficient to assure the complete irrigation of more than 100,000 acres south of Oroville and extending from the foothills of the Sierra Nevada Mountains far out into the Sacramento Valley.

The total development involves an expenditure of about $40,000,000.

And now comes the most unique phase of this most interesting development. The initial storage for this system will be secured by construction of a dam at the outlet of Gold Lake, the lake that tradition of the pioneers declares was sought in the Gold Lake stampede of the first Fifties, the most colorful and spectacular gold rush in California's history. A fantasy of yes-

terday, Gold Lake, albeit the gold is liquid, has become a reality of today.

Grizzly Valley, named because of the extent to which huge grizzly bears haunted it when the pioneers first came here, is another site selected by the Company for reservoir purposes.

But this is not all.

The operations of the Feather River Power Company through many miles of road construction, will make accessible an area that is declared to be exceeded in the magnificence of its beauty only by the Yosemite Valley.

This is the story. It is the story of Old U-I-NO conquered and of Bald Rock Canyon beaten and bound, not by the power of gold, but by the POWER of water dashing from the mountains to the valley below.

SAILORS NURSE MINERS

A burial in a '49 mining camp was simplicity itself,—as often, too, was death. If a miner was well, he was very well, but if sick, he was usually mighty sick. Doctors, such as they were, were very scarce and often difficult to locate. Of medicine there was little, either in variety or quantity.

Nearly every miner left the East with a supply of calomel pills, quinine powders and a box of arnica salve. In many instances these were used to excess, salivation followed, and the invalid lying on damp ground and on damp blankets was a very easy victim of pneumonia. The sailors were the Florence Nightingales of the mining camps, and their care saved many a miner from what appeared to be certain death.

No cemeteries were laid out at first the one and only essential of a burial place being that it be on ground free from gold.

The first industry of importance to follow the discovery of gold was lumbering. Timbers were needed for mining structures and soon lumbering became one of the major industries of the Feather River region. The pioneers accustomed to handling ox teams used the patient oxen as a means of transporting the timber from the pine forests to the mining camps. The view given above shows a typical lumbering scene of the Fifties with oxen hauling logs.

www.GoldMiningBooks.com

Books On Mining

Visit: www.goldminingbooks.com to order your copies or ask your favorite book seller to offer them.

Mining Books by Kerby Jackson

Gold Dust: Stories From Oregon's Mining Years - Oregon mining historian and prospector, Kerby Jackson, brings you a treasure trove of seventeen stories on Southern Oregon's rich history of gold prospecting, the prospectors and their discoveries, and the breathtaking areas they settled in and made homes. 5" X 8", 98 ppgs. Retail Price: $11.99

The Golden Trail: More Stories From Oregon's Mining Years - In his follow-up to "Gold Dust: Stories of Oregon's Mining Years", this time around, Jackson brings us twelve tales from Oregon's Gold Rush, including the story about the first gold strike on Canyon Creek in Grant County, about the old timers who found gold by the pail full at the Victor Mine near Galice, how Iradel Bray discovered a rich ledge of gold on the Coquille River during the height of the Rogue River War, a tale of two elderly miners on the hunt for a lost mine in the Cascade Mountains, details about the discovery of the famous Armstrong Nugget and others. 5" X 8", 70 ppgs. Retail Price: $10.99

Oregon Mining Books

Geology and Mineral Resources of Josephine County, Oregon - Unavailable since the 1970's, this important publication was originally compiled by the Oregon Department of Geology and Mineral Industries and includes important details on the economic geology and mineral resources of this important mining area in South Western Oregon. Included are notes on the history, geology and development of important mines, as well as insights into the mining of gold, copper, nickel, limestone, chromium and other minerals found in large quantities in Josephine County, Oregon. 8.5" X 11", 54 ppgs. Retail Price: $9.99

Mines and Prospects of the Mount Reuben Mining District - Unavailable since 1947, this important publication was originally compiled by geologist Elton Youngberg of the Oregon Department of Geology and Mineral Industries and includes detailed descriptions, histories and the geology of the Mount Reuben Mining District in Josephine County, Oregon. Included are notes on the history, geology, development and assay statistics, as well as underground maps of all the major mines and prospects in the vicinity of this much neglected mining district. 8.5" X 11", 48 ppgs. Retail Price: $9.99

The Granite Mining District - Notes on the history, geology and development of important mines in the well known Granite Mining District which is located in Grant County, Oregon. Some of the mines discussed include the Ajax, Blue Ribbon, Buffalo, Continental, Cougar-Independence, Magnolia, New York, Standard and the Tillicum. Also included are many rare maps pertaining to the mines in the area. 8.5" X 11", 48 ppgs. Retail Price: $9.99

Ore Deposits of the Takilma and Waldo Mining Districts of Josephine County, Oregon - The Waldo and Takilma mining districts are most notable for the fact that the earliest large scale mining of placer gold and copper in Oregon took place in these two areas. Included are details about some of the earliest large gold mines in the state such as the Llano de Oro, High Gravel, Cameron, Platerica, Deep Gravel and others, as well as copper mines such as the famous Queen of Bronze mine, the Waldo, Lily and Cowboy mines. This volume also includes six maps and 20 original illustrations. 8.5" X 11", 74 ppgs. Retail Price: $9.99

Metal Mines of Douglas, Coos and Curry Counties, Oregon - Oregon mining historian Kerby Jackson introduces us to a classic work on Oregon's mining history in this important re-issue of Bulletin 14C Volume 1, otherwise known as the Douglas, Coos & Curry Counties, Oregon Metal Mines Handbook. Unavailable since 1940, this important publication was originally compiled by the Oregon Department of Geology and Mineral Industries includes detailed descriptions, histories and the geology of over 250 metallic mineral mines and prospects in this rugged area of South West Oregon. 8.5" X 11", 158 ppgs. Retail Price: $19.99

Metal Mines of Jackson County, Oregon - Unavailable since 1943, this important publication was originally compiled by the Oregon Department of Geology and Mineral Industries includes detailed descriptions, histories and the geology of over 450 metallic mineral mines and prospects in Jackson County, Oregon. Included are such famous gold mining areas as Gold Hill, Jacksonville, Sterling and the Upper Applegate. **8.5" X 11", 220 ppgs. Retail Price: $24.99**

Metal Mines of Josephine County, Oregon - Oregon mining historian Kerby Jackson introduces us to a classic work on Oregon's mining history in this important re-issue of Bulletin 14C, otherwise known as the Josephine County, Oregon Metal Mines Handbook. Unavailable since 1952, this important publication was originally compiled by the Oregon Department of Geology and Mineral Industries includes detailed descriptions, histories and the geology of over 500 metallic mineral mines and prospects in Josephine County, Oregon. **8.5" X 11", 250 ppgs. Retail Price: $24.99**

Metal Mines of North East Oregon - Oregon mining historian Kerby Jackson introduces us to a classic work on Oregon's mining history in this important re-issue of Bulletin 14A and 14B, otherwise known as the North East Oregon Metal Mines Handbook. Unavailable since 1941, this important publication was originally compiled by the Oregon Department of Geology and Mineral Industries and includes detailed descriptions, histories and the geology of over 750 metallic mineral mines and prospects in North Eastern Oregon. **8.5" X 11", 310 ppgs. Retail Price: $29.99**

Metal Mines of North West Oregon - Oregon mining historian Kerby Jackson introduces us to a classic work on Oregon's mining history in this important re-issue of Bulletin 14D, otherwise known as the North West Oregon Metal Mines Handbook. Unavailable since 1951, this important publication was originally compiled by the Oregon Department of Geology and Mineral Industries and includes detailed descriptions, histories and the geology of over 250 metallic mineral mines and prospects in North Western Oregon. **8.5" X 11", 182 ppgs. Retail Price: $19.99**

Mines and Prospects of Oregon - Mining historian Kerby Jackson introduces us to a classic mining work by the Oregon Bureau of Mines in this important re-issue of The Handbook of Mines and Prospects of Oregon. Unavailable since 1916, this publication includes important insights into hundreds of gold, silver, copper, coal, limestone and other mines that operated in the State of Oregon around the turn of the 19th Century. Included are not only geological details on early mines throughout Oregon, but also insights into their history, production, locations and in some cases, also included are rare maps of their underground workings. **8.5" X 11", 314 ppgs. Retail Price: $24.99**

Lode Gold of the Klamath Mountains of Northern California and South West Oregon
(See California Mining Books)

Mineral Resources of South West Oregon - Unavailable since 1914, this publication includes important insights into dozens of mines that once operated in South West Oregon, including the famous gold fields of Josephine and Jackson Counties, as well as the Coal Mines of Coos County. Included are not only geological details on early mines throughout South West Oregon, but also insights into their history, production and locations. **8.5" X 11", 154 ppgs. Retail Price: $11.99**

Chromite Mining in The Klamath Mountains of California and Oregon
(See California Mining Books)

Southern Oregon Mineral Wealth - Unavailable since 1904, this rare publication provides a unique snapshot into the mines that were operating in the area at the time. Included are not only geological details on early mines throughout South West Oregon, but also insights into their history, production and locations. Some of the mining areas include Grave Creek, Greenback, Wolf Creek, Jump Off Joe Creek, Granite Hill, Galice, Mount Reuben, Gold Hill, Galls Creek, Kane Creek, Sardine Creek, Birdseye Creek, Evans Creek, Foots Creek, Jacksonville, Ashland, the Applegate River, Waldo, Kerby and the Illinois River, Althouse and Sucker Creek, as well as insights into local copper mining and other topics. **8.5" X 11", 64 ppgs. Retail Price: $8.99**

Geology and Ore Deposits of the Takilma and Waldo Mining Districts - Unavailable since the 1933, this publication was originally compiled by the United States Geological Survey and includes details on gold and copper mining in the Takilma and Waldo Districts of Josephine County, Oregon. The Waldo and Takilma mining districts are most notable for the fact that the earliest large scale mining of placer gold and copper in Oregon took place in these two areas. Included in this report are details about some of the earliest large gold mines in the state such as the Llano de Oro, High Gravel, Cameron, Platerica, Deep Gravel and others, as well as copper mines such as the famous Queen of Bronze mine, the Waldo, Lily and Cowboy mines. In addition to geological examinations, insights are also provided into the production, day to day operations and early histories of these mines, as well as calculations of known mineral reserves in the area. This volume also includes six maps and 20 original illustrations. **8.5" X 11", 74 ppgs. Retail Price: $9.99**

Gold Mines of Oregon - Oregon mining historian Kerby Jackson introduces us to a classic work on Oregon's mining history in this important re-issue of Bulletin 61, otherwise known as "Gold and Silver In Oregon". Unavailable since 1968, this important publication was originally compiled by geologists Howard C. Brooks and Len Ramp of the Oregon Department of Geology and Mineral Industries and includes detailed descriptions, histories and the geology of over 450 gold mines Oregon. Included are notes on the history, geology and gold production statistics of all the major mining areas in Oregon including the Klamath Mountains, the Blue Mountains and the North Cascades. While gold is where you find it, as every miner knows, the path to success is to prospect for gold where it was previously found. **8.5" X 11", 344 ppgs. Retail Price: $24.99**

Mines and Mineral Resources of Curry County Oregon - Originally published in 1916, this important publication on Oregon Mining has not been available for nearly a century. Included are rare insights into the history, production and locations of dozens of gold mines in Curry County, Oregon, as well as detailed information on important Oregon mining districts in that area such as those at Agness, Bald Face Creek, Mule Creek, Boulder Creek, China Diggings, Collier Creek, Elk River, Gold Beach, Rock Creek, Sixes River and elsewhere. Particular attention is especially paid to the famous beach gold deposits of this portion of the Oregon Coast. **8.5" X 11", 140 ppgs. Retail Price: $11.99**

Chromite Mining in South West Oregon - Originally published in 1961, this important publication on Oregon Mining has not been available for nearly a century. Included are rare insights into the history, production and locations of nearly 300 chromite mines in South Western Oregon. **8.5" X 11", 184 ppgs. Retail Price: $14.99**

Mineral Resources of Douglas County Oregon - Originally published in 1972, this important publication on Oregon Mining has not been available for nearly forty years. Included are rare insights into the geology, history, production and locations of numerous gold mines and other mining properties in Douglas County, Oregon. **8.5" X 11", 124 ppgs. Retail Price: $11.99**

Mineral Resources of Coos County Oregon - Originally published in 1972, this important publication on Oregon Mining has not been available for nearly forty years. Included are rare insights into the geology, history, production and locations of numerous gold mines and other mining properties in Coos County, Oregon. **8.5" X 11", 100 ppgs. Retail Price: $11.99**

Mineral Resources of Lane County Oregon - Originally published in 1938, this important publication on Oregon Mining has not been available for nearly seventy five years. Included are extremely rare insights into the geology and mines of Lane County, Oregon, in particular in the Bohemia, Blue River, Oakridge, Black Butte and Winberry Mining Districts. **8.5" X 11", 82 ppgs. Retail Price: $9.99**

Mineral Resources of the Upper Chetco River of Oregon: Including the Kalmiopsis Wilderness - Originally published in 1975, this important publication on Oregon Mining has not been available for nearly forty years. Withdrawn under the 1872 Mining Act since 1984, real insight into the minerals resources and mines of the Upper Chetco River has long been unavailable due to the remoteness of the area. Despite this, the decades of battle between property owners and environmental extremists over the last private mining inholding in the area has continued to pique the interest of those interested in mining and other forms of natural resource use. Gold mining began in the area in the 1850's and has a rich history in this geographic area, even if the facts surrounding it are little known. Included are twenty two rare photographs, as well as insights into the Becca and Morning Mine, the Emmly Mine (also known as Emily Camp), the Frazier Mine, the Golden Dream or Higgins Mine, Hustis Mine, Peck Mine and others. **8.5" X 11", 64 ppgs. Retail Price: $8.99**

Gold Dredging in Oregon - Originally published in 1939, this important publication on Oregon Mining has not been available for nearly seventy five years. Included are extremely rare insights into the history and day to day operations of the dragline and bucketline gold dredges that once worked the placer gold fields of South West and North East Oregon in decades gone by. Also included are details into the areas that were worked by gold dredges in Josephine, Jackson, Baker and Grant counties, as well as the economic factors that impacted this mining method. This volume also offers a unique look into the values of river bottom land in relation to both farming and mining, in how farm lands were mined, re-soiled and reclamated after the dredges worked them. Featured are hard to find maps of the gold dredge fields, as well as rare photographs from a bygone era. **8.5" X 11", 86 ppgs. Retail Price: $8.99**

Quick Silver Mining in Oregon - Originally published in 1963, this important publication on Oregon Mining has not been available for over fifty years. This publication includes details into the history and production of Elemental Mercury or Quicksilver in the State of Oregon. **8.5" X 11", 238 ppgs. Retail Price: $15.99**

Mines of the Greenhorn Mining District of Grant County Oregon - Originally published in 1948, this important publication on Oregon Mining has not been available for over sixty five years. In this publication are rare insights into the mines of the famous Greenhorn Mining District of Grant County, Oregon, especially the famous Morning Mine. Also included are details on the Tempest, Tiger, Bi-Metallic, Windsor, Psyche, Big Johnny, Snow Creek, Banzette and Paramount Mines, as well as prospects in the vicinities in the famous mining areas of Mormon Basin, Vinegar Basin and Desolation Creek. Included are hard to find mine maps and dozens of rare photographs from the bygone era of Grant County's rich mining history. **8.5" X 11", 72 ppgs. Retail Price: $9.99**

Geology of the Wallowa Mountains of Oregon: Part I (Volume 1) - Originally published in 1938, this important publication on Oregon Mining has not been available for nearly seventy five years. Included are details on the geology of this unique portion of North Eastern Oregon. This is the first part of a two book series on the area. Accompanying the text are rare photographs and historic maps.**8.5" X 11", 92 ppgs. Retail Price: $9.99**

Geology of the Wallowa Mountains of Oregon: Part II (Volume 2) - Originally published in 1938, this important publication on Oregon Mining has not been available for nearly seventy five years. Included are details on the geology of this unique portion of North Eastern Oregon. This is the first part of a two book series on the area. Accompanying the text are rare photographs and historic maps.**8.5" X 11", 94 ppgs. Retail Price: $9.99**

Field Identification of Minerals For Oregon Prospectors - Originally published in 1940, this important publication on Oregon Mining has not been available for nearly seventy five years. Included in this volume is an easy system for testing and identifying a wide range of minerals that might be found by prospectors, geologists and rockhounds in the State of Oregon, as well as in other locales. Topics include how to put together your own field testing kit and how to conduct rudimentary tests in the field. This volume is written in a clear and concise way to make it useful even for beginners. **8.5" X 11", 158 ppgs. Retail Price: $14.99**

The Bohemia Mining District of Oregon - Originally published in 1900, this important publication on Oregon Mining has not been available for over a century. Included in this volume are important insights into the famous Bohemia Mining District of Oregon, including the histories and locations of important gold mines in the area such as the Ophir Mine, Clarence, Acturas, Peek-a-boo, White Swan, Combination Mine, the Musick Mine, The California, White Ghost, The Mystery, Wall Street, Vesuvius, Story, Lizzie Bullock, Delta, Elsie Dora, Golden Slipper, Broadway, Champion Mine, Knott, Noonday, Helena, White Wings, Riverside and others. Also included are notes on the nearby Blue River Mining District. **8.5" X 11", 58 ppgs. Retail Price: $9.99**

The Gold Fields of Eastern Oregon - Unavailable since 1900, this publication was originally compiled by the Baker City Chamber of Commerce Offering important insights into the gold mining history of Eastern Oregon, "The Gold Fields of Eastern Oregon" sheds a rare light on many of the gold mines that were operating at the turn of the 19th Century in Baker County and Grant County in North Eastern Oregon. Some of the areas featured include the Cable Cove District, Baisely-Elhorn, Granite, Red Boy, Bonanza, Susanville, Sparta, Virtue, Vaughn, Sumpter, Burnt River, Rye Valley and other mining districts. Included is basic information on not only many gold mines that are well known to those interested in Eastern Oregon mining history, but also many mines and prospects which have been mostly lost to the passage of time. Accompanying are numerous rare photos **8.5" X 11", 78 ppgs. Retail Price: $10.99**

Gold Mining in Eastern Oregon - Originally published in 1938, this important publication on Oregon Mining has not been available for over a century. Included in this volume are important insights into the famous mining districts of Eastern Oregon during the late 1930's. Particular attention is given to those gold mines with milling and concentrating facilities in the Greenhorn, Red Boy, Alamo, Bonanza, Granite, Cable Cove, Cracker Creek, Virtue, Keating, Medical Springs, Sanger, Sparta, Chicken Creek, Mormon Basin, Connor Creek, Cornucopia and the Bull Run Mining Districts. Some of the mines featured include the Ben Harrison, North Pole-Columbia, Highland Maxwell, Baisley-Elkhorn, White Swan, Balm Creek, Twin Baby, Gem of Sparta, New Deal, Gleason, Gifford-Johnson, Cornucopia, Record, Bull Run, Orion and others. Of particular interest are the mill flow sheets and descriptions of milling operations of these mines. **8.5" X 11", 68 ppgs. Retail Price: $8.99**

The Gold Belt of the Blue Mountains of Oregon - Originally published in 1901, this important publication on Oregon Mining has not been available for over a century. Included in this volume are rare insights into the gold deposits of the Blue Mountains of North East Oregon, including the history of their early discovery and early production. Extensive details are offered on this important mining area's mineralogy and economic geology, as well as insights into nearby gold placers, silver deposits and copper deposits. Featured are the Elkhorn and Rock Creek mining districts, the Pocahontas district, Auburn and Minersville districts, Sumpter and Cracker Creek, Cable Cove, the Camp Carson district, Granite, Alamo, Greenhorn, Robinsonville, the Upper Burnt River Valley and Bonanza districts, Susanville, Quartzburg, Canyon Creek, Virtue, the Copper Butte district, the North Powder River, Sparta, Eagle Creek, Cornucopia, Pine Creek, Lower Powder River, the Upper Snake River Canyon, Rye Valley, Lower Burnt River Valley, Mormon Basin, the Malheur and Clarks Creek districts, Sutton Creek and others. Of particular interest are important details on numerous gold mines and prospects in these mining districts, including their locations, histories, geology and other important information, as well as information on silver, copper and fire opal deposits. **8.5" X 11", 250 ppgs. Retail Price: $24.99**

Mining in the Cascades Range of Oregon - Originally published in 1938, this important publication on Oregon Mining has not been available for over seventy five years. Included in this volume are rare insights into the gold mines and other types of metal mines in the Cascades Mountain Range of Oregon. Some of the important mining areas covered include the famous Bohemia Mining District, the North Santiam Mining District, Quartzville Mining District, Blue River Mining District, Fall Creek Mining District, Oakridge District, Zinc District, Buzzard-Al Sarena District, Grand Cove, Climax District and Barron Mining District. Of particular interest are important details on over 100 mines and prospects in these mining districts, including their locations, histories, geology and other important information. **8.5" X 11", 170 ppgs. Retail Price: $14.99**

Beach Gold Placers of the Oregon Coast - Originally published in 1934, this important publication on Oregon Mining has not been available for over 80 years. Included in this volume are rare insights into the beach gold deposits of the State of Oregon, including their locations, occurance, composition and geology. Of particular interest is information on placer platinum in Oregon's rich beach deposits. Also included are the locations and other information on some famous Oregon beach mines, including the Pioneer, Eagle, Chickamin, Iowa and beach placer mines north of the mouth of the Rogue River. **8.5" X 11", 60 ppgs. Retail Price: $8.99**

Idaho Mining Books

Gold in Idaho - Unavailable since the 1940's, this publication was originally compiled by the Idaho Bureau of Mines and includes details on gold mining in Idaho. Included is not only raw data on gold production in Idaho, but also valuable insight into where gold may be found in Idaho, as well as practical information on the gold bearing rocks and other geological features that will assist those looking for placer and lode gold in the State of Idaho. This volume also includes thirteen gold maps that greatly enhance the practical usability of the information contained in this small book detailing where to find gold in Idaho. **8.5" X 11", 72 ppgs. Retail Price: $9.99**

Geology of the Couer D'Alene Mining District of Idaho - Unavailable since 1961, this publication was originally compiled by the Idaho Bureau of Mines and Geology and includes details on the mining of gold, silver and other minerals in the famous Coeur D'Alene Mining District in Northern Idaho. Included are details on the early history of the Coeur D'Alene Mining District, local tectonic settings, ore deposit features, information on the mineral belts of the Osburn Fault, as well as detailed information on the famous Bunker Hill Mine, the Dayrock Mine, Galena Mine, Lucky Friday Mine and the infamous Sunshine Mine. This volume also includes sixteen hard to find maps. **8.5" X 11", 70 ppgs. Retail Price: $9.99**

The Gold Camps and Silver Cities of Idaho - Originally published in 1963, this important publication on Idaho Mining has not been available for nearly fifty years. Included are rare insights into the history of Idaho's Gold Rush, as well as the mad craze for silver in the Idaho Panhandle. Documented in fine detail are the early mining excitements at Boise Basin, at South Boise, in the Owyhees, at Deadwood, Long Valley, Stanley Basin and Robinson Bar, at Atlanta, on the famous Boise River, Volcano, Little Smokey, Banner, Boise Ridge, Hailey, Leesburg, Lemhi, Pearl, at South Mountain, Shoup and Ulysses, Yellow Jacket and Loon Creek. The story follows with the appearance of Chinese miners at the new mining camps on the Snake River, Black Pine, Yankee Fork, Bay Horse, Clayton, Heath, Seven Devils, Gibbonsville, Vienna and Sawtooth City. Also included are special sections on the Idaho Lead and Silver mines of the late 1800's, as well as the mining discoveries of the early 1900's that paved the way for Idaho's modern mining and mineral industry. Lavishly illustrated with rare historic photos, this volume provides a one of a kind documentary into Idaho's mining history that is sure to be enjoyed by not only modern miners and prospectors who still scour the hills in search of nature's treasures, but also those enjoy history and tromping through overgrown ghost towns and long abandoned mining camps. **8.5" X 11", 186 ppgs. Retail Price: $14.99**

Ore Deposits and Mining in North Western Custer County Idaho - Unavailable since 1913, this important publication was originally published by the Us Department of the Interior and has been unavailable for a century. Included are fine details on the geology, geography, gold placers and gold and silver bearing quartz veins of the mining region of North West Custer County, Idaho. Of particular interest is a rare look at the mines and prospects of the region, including those such as the Ramshorn Mine, SkyLark, Riverview, Excelsior, Beardsley, Pacific, Hoosier, Silver Brick, Forest Rose and dozens of others in the Bay Horse Mining District. Also covered are the mines of the Yankee Fork District such as the Lucky Boy, Badger, Black, Enterprise, Charles Dickens, Morrison, Golden Sunbeam, Montana, Golden Gate and others, as well as those in the Loon Mining District. **8.5" X 11", 126 ppgs. Retail Price: $12.99**

Gold Rush To Idaho - Unavailable since 1963, this important publication was originally published by the Idaho Bureau of Mines and has been unavailable for 50 years. "Gold Rush To Idaho" revisits the earliest years of the discovery of gold in Idaho Territory and introduces us to the conditions that the pioneer gold seekers met when they blazed a trail through the wilderness of Idaho's mountains and discovered the precious yellow metal at Oro Fino and Pierce. Subsequent rushes followed at places like Elk City, Newsome, Clearwater Station, Florence, Warrens and elsewhere. Of particular interest is a rare look at the hardships that the first miners in Idaho met with during their day to day existences and their attempts to bring law and order to their mining camps. **8.5" X 11", 88 ppgs. Retail Price: $9.99**

The Geology and Mines of Northern Idaho and North Western Montana - Unavailable since 1909, this important publication was originally published by the Us Department of the Interior and has been unavailable for a century. Included are fine details on the geology and geography of the mining regions of Northern Idaho and North Western Montana. Of particular interest is a rare look at the mines and prospects of the region, including those in the Pine Creek Mining District, Lake Pend Oreille district, Troy Mining District, Sylvanite District, Cabinet Mining District, Prospect Mining District and the Missoula Valley. Some of the mines featured include the Iron Mountain, Silver Butte, Snowshoe, Grouse Mountain Mine and others. **8.5" X 11", 142 ppgs. Retail Price: $12.99**

Mining in the Alturas Quadrangle of Blaine County Idaho - Unavailable since 1922, this important publication was originally published by the Idaho Bureau of Mines and has been unavailable for ninety years. Topics include the geology, rock formations and the formation of ore deposits in this important mining area of Idaho. Of particular focus is information on the local geology, quartz veins and ore deposits of this portion of Idaho. Included are hard to find details, including the descriptions and locations of numerous gold and silver mines in the area including the Silver King, Pilgrim, Columbia, Lone Jack, Sunbeam, Pride of the West, Lucky Boy, Scotia, Atlanta, Beaver-Bidwell and others mines and prospects. **8.5" X 11", 56 ppgs. Retail Price: $8.99**

Mining in Lemhi County Idaho - Originally published in 1913, this important book on Idaho Mining has not been available to miners for over a century. Included are rare insights into hundreds of gold, silver, copper and other mines in this famous Idaho mining area. Details include the locations, geology, history, production and other facts of the mines of this region, not only gold and silver hardrock mines, but also gold placer mines, lead-silver deposits, copper mines, cobalt-nickel deposits, tungsten and tin mines . It is lavishly illustrated with hard to find photos of the period and rare mining maps. Some of the vicinities featured include the Nicholia Mining District, Spring Mountain District, Texas District, Blue Wing District, Junction District, McDevitt District, Pratt Creek, Eldorado District, Kirtley Creek, Carmen Creek, Gibbonsville, Indian Creek, Mineral Hill District, Mackinaw, Eureka District, Blackbird District, YellowJacket District, Gravel Range District, Junction District, Parker Mountain and other mining districts. **8.5" X 11", 226 ppgs. Retail Price: $19.99**

Utah Mining Books

Fluorite in Utah - Unavailable since 1954, this publication was originally compiled by the USGS, State of Utah and U.S. Atomic Energy Commission and details the mining of fluorspar, also known as fluorite in the State of Utah. Included are details on the geology and history of fluorspar (fluorite) mining in Utah, including details on where this unique gem mineral may be found in the State of Utah. **8.5" X 11", 60 ppgs. Retail Price: $8.99**

California Mining Books

The Tertiary Gravels of the Sierra Nevada of California - Mining historian Kerby Jackson introduces us to a classic mining work by Waldemar Lindgren in this important re-issue of The Tertiary Gravels of the Sierra Nevada of California. Unavailable since 1911, this publication includes details on the gold bearing ancient river channels of the famous Sierra Nevada region of California. **8.5" X 11", 282 ppgs. Retail Price: $19.99**

The Mother Lode Mining Region of California - Unavailable since 1900, this publication includes details on the gold mines of California's famous Mother Lode gold mining area. Included are details on the geology, history and important gold mines of the region, as well as insights into historic mining methods, mine timbering, mining machinery, mining bell signals and other details on how these mines operated. Also included are insights into the gold mines of the California Mother Lode that were in operation during the first sixty years of California's mining history. **8.5" X 11", 176 ppgs. Retail Price: $14.99**

Lode Gold of the Klamath Mountains of Northern California and South West Oregon - Unavailable since 1971, this publication was originally compiled by Preston E. Hotz and includes details on the lode mining districts of Oregon and California's Klamath Mountains. Included are details on the geology, history and important lode mines of the French Gulch, Deadwood, Whiskeytown, Shasta, Redding, Muletown, South Fork, Old Diggings, Dog Creek (Delta), Bully Choop (Indian Creek), Harrison Gulch, Hayfork, Minersville, Trinity Center, Canyon Creek, East Fork, New River, Denny, Liberty (Black Bear), Cecilville, Callahan, Yreka, Fort Jones and Happy Camp mining districts in California, as well as the Ashland, Rogue River, Applegate, Illinois River, Takilma, Greenback, Galice, Silver Peak, Myrtle Creek and Mule Creek districts of South Western Oregon. Also included are insights into the mineralization and other characteristics of this important mining region. **8.5" X 11", 100 ppgs. Retail Price: $10.99**

Mines and Mineral Resources of Shasta County, Siskiyou County, Trinity County: California - Unavailable since 1915, this publication was originally compiled by the California State Mining Bureau and includes details on the gold mines of this area of Northern California. Also included are insights into the mineralization and other characteristics of this important mining region, as well as the location of historic gold mines. 8.5" X 11", 204 ppgs. Retail Price: $19.99

Geology of the Yreka Quadrangle, Siskiyou County, California - Unavailable since 1977, this publication was originally compiled by Preston E. Hotz and includes details on the geology of the Yreka Quadrangle of Siskiyou County, California. Also included are insights into the mineralization and other characteristics of this important mining region. 8.5" X 11", 78 ppgs. Retail Price: $7.99

Mines of San Diego and Imperial Counties, California - Originally published in 1914, this important publication on California Mining has not been available for a century. This publication includes important information on the early gold mines of San Diego and Imperial County, which were some of the first gold fields mined in California by early Spanish and Mexican miners before the 49ers came on the scene. Included are not only details on early mining methods in the area, production statistics and geological information, but also the location of the early gold mines that helped make California "The Golden State". Also included are details on the mining of other minerals such as silver, lead, zinc, manganese, tungsten, vanadium, asbestos, barite, borax, cement, clay, dolomite, fluospar, gem stones, graphite, marble, salines, petroleum, stronium, talc and others. 8.5" X 11", 116 ppgs. Retail Price: $12.99

Mines of Sierra County, California - Unavailable since 1920, this publication was originally compiled by the California State Mining Bureau and includes details on the gold mines of Sierra County, California. Also included are insights into the mineralization and other characteristics of this important mining region, as well as the location of historic gold mines. 8.5" X 11", 156 ppgs. Retail Price: $19.99

Mines of Plumas County, California - Unavailable since 1918, this publication was originally compiled by the California State Mining Bureau and includes details on the gold mines of Plumas County, California. Also included are insights into the mineralization and other characteristics of this important mining region, as well as the location of historic gold mines. 8.5" X 11", 200 ppgs. Retail Price: $19.99

Mines of El Dorado, Placer, Sacramento and Yuba Counties, California - Originally published in 1917, this important publication on California Mining has not been available for nearly a century. This publication includes important information on the early gold mines of El Dorado County, Placer County, Sacramento County and Yuba County, which were some of the first gold fields mined by the Forty-Niners during the California Gold Rush. Included are not only details on early mining methods in the area, production statistics and geological information, but also the location of the early gold mines that helped make California "The Golden State". Also included are insights into the early mining of chrome, copper and other minerals in this important mining area. 8.5" X 11", 204 ppgs. Retail Price: $19.99

Mines of Los Angeles, Orange and Riverside Counties, California - Originally published in 1917, this important publication on California Mining has not been available for nearly a century. This publication includes important information on the early gold mines of Los Angeles County, Orange County and Riverside County, which were some of the first gold fields mined in California by early Spanish and Mexican miners before the 49ers came on the scene. Included are not only details on early mining methods in the area, production statistics and geological information, but also the location of the early gold mines that helped make California "The Golden State". 8.5" X 11", 146 ppgs. Retail Price: $12.99

Mines of San Bernadino and Tulare Counties, California - Originally published in 1917, this important publication on California Mining has not been available for nearly a century. This publication includes important information on the early gold mines of San Bernadino and Tulare County, which were some of the first gold fields mined in California by early Spanish and Mexican miners before the 49ers came on the scene. Included are not only details on early mining methods in the area, production statistics and geological information, but also the location of the early gold mines that helped make California "The Golden State". Also included are details on the mining of other minerals such as copper, iron, lead, zinc, manganese, tungsten, vanadium, asbestos, barite, borax, cement, clay, dolomite, fluospar, gem stones, graphite, marble, salines, petroleum, stronium, talc and others. 8.5" X 11", 200 ppgs. Retail Price: $19.99

Chromite Mining in The Klamath Mountains of California and Oregon - Unavailable since 1919, this publication was originally compiled by J.S. Diller of the United States Department of Geological Survey and includes details on the chromite mines of this area of Northern California and Southern Oregon. Also included are insights into the mineralization and other characteristics of this important mining region, as well as the location of historic mines. Also included are insights into chromite mining in Eastern Oregon and Montana. 8.5" X 11", 98 ppgs. Retail Price: $9.99

Mines and Mining in Amador, Calaveras and Tuolumne Counties, California - Unavailable since 1915, this publication was originally compiled by William Tucker and includes details on the mines and mineral resources of this important California mining area. Included are details on the geology, history and important gold mines of the region, as well as insights into other local mineral resources such as asbestos, clay, copper, talc, limestone and others. Also included are insights into the mineralization and other characteristics of this important portion of California's Mother Lode mining region. **8.5" X 11", 198 ppgs. Retail Price: $14.99**

The Cerro Gordo Mining District of Inyo County California - Unavailable since 1963, this publication was originally compiled by the United States Department of Interior. Included are insights into the mineralization and other characteristics of this important mining region of Southern California. Topics include the mining of gold and silver in this important mining district in Inyo County, California, including details on the history, production and locations of the Cerro Gordo Mine, the Morning Star Mine, Estelle Tunnel, Charles Lease Tunnel, Ignacio, Hart, Crosscut Tunnel, Sunset, Upper Newtown, Newtown, Ella, Perseverance, Newsboy, Belmont and other silver and gold mines in the Cerro Gordo Mining District. This volume also includes important insights into the fossil record, geologic formations, faults and other aspects of economic geology in this California mining district. **8.5" X 11", 104 ppgs. Retail Price: $10.99**

Mining in Butte, Lassen, Modoc, Sutter and Tehama Counties of California - Unavailable since 1917, this publication was originally compiled by the United States Department of Interior. Included are insights into the mineralization and other characteristics of this important mining region of California. Topics include the mining of asbestos, chromite, gold, diamonds and manganese in Butte County, the mining of gold and copper in the Hayden Hill and Diamond Mountain mining districts of Lassen County, the mining of coal, salt, copper and gold in the High Grade and Winters mining districts of Modoc County, gold mining in Sutter County and the mining of gold, chromite, manganese and copper in Tehama County. This volume also includes the production records and locations of numerous mines in this important mining region. **8.5" X 11", 114 ppgs. Retail Price: $11.99**

Mines of Trinity County California - Originally published in 1965, this important publication on California Mining has not been available for nearly fifty years. This publication includes important information on mines and mining in Trinity County, California, as well insights into the mineralization and geology of this important mining area in Northern California. Included are extensive details on hardrock and placer gold mines and prospects, including charts showing the locations of these historic mines.. **8.5" X 11", 144 ppgs. Retail Price: $12.99**

Mines of Kern County California - Originally published in 1962, this important publication on California Mining has not been available for nearly fifty years. This publication includes important information on mines and mining in Kern County, California, as well insights into the mineralization and geology of this important mining area in California. Included are extensive details on hardrock and placer gold mines and prospects, including charts showing the locations of these historic mines. **8.5" X 11", 398 ppgs. Retail Price: $24.99**

Mines of Calaveras County California - Originally published in 1962, this important publication on California Mining has not been available for nearly fifty years. This publication includes important information on mines and mining in Calaveras County, California, as well insights into the mineralization and geology of this important mining area in Northern California. Included are extensive details on hardrock and placer gold mines and prospects, including charts showing the locations of these historic mines. **8.5" X 11", 236 ppgs. Retail Price: $19.99**

Lode Gold Mining in Grass Valley California - Unavailable since 1940, this publication was originally compiled by the United States Department of Interior. Included are insights into the gold mineralization and other characteristics of this important mining region of Nevada County, California. This volume also includes important insights into the geologic formations, faults and other aspects of economic geology in this California mining district. Of particular interest are the fine details on many hardrock gold mines in the area, including their locations, histories, development and mineralization. Some of the mines featured include the Gold Hill Mine, Massachusetts Hill, Boundary, Peabody, Golden Center, North Star, Omaha, Lone Jack, Homeward Bound, Hartery, Wisconsin, Allison Ranch, Phoenix, Kate Hayes, W.Y.O.D., Empire, Rich Hill, Daisy Hill, Orleans, Sultana, Centennial, Conlin, Ben Franklin, Crown Point and many others. **8.5" X 11", 148 ppgs. Retail Price: $12.99**

Lode Mining in the Alleghany District of Sierra County California - Unavailable since 1913, this publication was originally compiled by the United States Department of Interior. Included are insights into the mineralization and other characteristics of this important mining region of Sierra County. Included are details on the history, production and locations of numerous hardrock gold mines in this famous California area, including the Tightner Mine, Minnie D., Osceola, Eldorado, Twenty One, Sherman, Kenton, Oriental, Rainbow, Plumbago, Irelan, Gold Canyon, North Fork, Federal, Kate Hardy and others. This volume also includes important insights into the fossil record, geologic formations, faults and other aspects of economic geology in this California mining district. **8.5" X 11", 48 ppgs. Retail Price: $7.99**

Six Months In The Gold Mines During The California Gold Rush - Unavailable since 1850, this important work is a first hand account of one "49'ers" personal experience during the great California Gold Rush, shedding important light on one of the most exciting periods in the history of not only California, but also the world. Compiled from journals written between 1847 and 1849 by E. Gould Buffum, a native of New York, "Six Months In The Gold Mines During The California Gold Rush" offers a rare look into the day to day lives of the people who came to California to work in her gold mines when the state was still a great frontier. **8.5" X 11", 290 ppgs. Retail Price: $19.99**

Quartz Mines of the Grass Valley Mining District of California - Unavailable since 1867, this important publication has not been available since those days. This rare publication offers a short dissertation on the early hardrock mines in this important mining district in the California Mother Lode region between the 1850's and 1860's. Also included are hard to find details on the mineralization and locations of these mines, as well as how they were operated in those day. **8.5" X 11", 44 ppgs. Retail Price: $8.99**

Alaska Mining Books

Ore Deposits of the Willow Creek Mining District, Alaska - Unavailable since 1954, this hard to find publication includes valuable insights into the Willow Creek Mining District near Hatcher Pass in Alaska. The publication includes insights into the history, geology and locations of the well known mines in the area, including the Gold Cord, Independence, Fern, Mabel, Lonesome, Snowbird, Schroff-O'Neil, High Grade, Marion Twin, Thorpe, Webfoot, Kelly-Willow, Lane, Holland and others. **8.5" X 11", 96 ppgs. Retail Price: $9.99**

The Juneau Gold Belt of Alaska - Unavailable since 1906, this hard to find publication includes valuable insights into the gold mines around Juneau, Alaska. The publication includes important details into the history, geology and locations of the well known gold mines and prospects in the area, including those around Windham Bay, Holkham Bay, Port Snettisham, on Grindstone and Rhine Creeks, Gold Creek, Douglas Island, Salmon Creek, Lemon Creek, Nugget Creek, from the Mendenhall River to Berners Bay, McGinnis Creek, Montana Creek, Peterson Creek, Windfall Creek, the Eagle River, Yankee Basin, Yankee Curve, Kowee Creek and elsewhere. Not only are gold placer mines included, but also hardrock gold mines. **8.5" X 11", 224 ppgs. Retail Price: $19.99**

Arizona Mining Books

Mines and Mining in Northern Yuma County Arizona - Originally published in 1911, this important publication on Arizona Mining has not been available for over a hundred years. Included are rare insights into the gold, silver, copper and quicksilver mines of Yuma County, Arizona together with hard to find maps and photographs. Some of the mines and mining districts featured include the Planet Copper Mine, Mineral Hill, the Clara Consolidated Mine, Viati Mine, Copper Basin prospect, Bowman Mine, Quartz King, Billy Mack, Carnation, the Wardwell and Osbourne, Valensuella Copper, the Mariquita, Colonial Mine, the French American, the New York-Plomosa, Guadalupe, Lead Camp, Mudersbach Copper Camp, Yellow Bird, the Arizona Northern (Salome Strike), Bonanza (Harqua Hala), Golden Eagle, Hercules, Socorro and others. **8.5" X 11", 144 ppgs. Retail Price: $11.99**

The Aravaipa and Stanley Mining Districts of Graham County Arizona - Originally published in 1925, this important publication on Arizona Mining has not been available for nearly ninety years. Included are rare insights into the gold and silver mines of these two important mining districts, together with hard to find maps. **8.5" X 11", 140 ppgs. Retail Price: $11.99**

Gold in the Gold Basin and Lost Basin Mining Districts of Mohave County, Arizona - This volume contains rare insights into the geology and gold mineralization of the Gold Basin and Lost Basin Mining Districts of Mohave County, Arizona that will be of benefit to miners and prospectors. Also included is a significant body of information on the gold mines and prospects of this portion of Arizona. This volume is lavishly illustrated with rare photos and mining maps. **8.5" X 11", 188 ppgs. Retail Price: $19.99**

Mines of the Jerome and Bradshaw Mountains of Arizona - This important publication on Arizona Mining has not been available for ninety years. This volume contains rare insights into the geology and ore deposits of the Jerome and Bradshaw Mountains of Arizona that will be of benefit to miners and prospectors who work those areas. Included is a significant body of information on the mines and prospects of the Verde, Black Hills, Cherry Creek, Prescott, Walker, Groom Creek, Hassayampa, Bigbug, Turkey Creek, Agua Fria, Black Canyon, Peck, Tiger, Pine Grove, Bradshaw, Tintop, Humbug and Castle Creek Mining Districts. This volume is lavishly illustrated with rare photos and mining maps. **8.5" X 11", 218 ppgs. Retail Price: $19.99**

The Ajo Mining District of Pima County Arizona - This important publication on Arizona Mining has not been available for nearly seventy years. This volume contains rare insights into the geology and mineralization of the Ajo Mining District in Pima County, Arizona and in particular the famous New Cornelia Mine. **8.5" X 11", 126 ppgs. Retail Price: $11.99**

Mining in the Santa Rita and Patagonia Mountains of Arizona - Originally published in 1915, this important publication on Arizona Mining has not been available for nearly a century. Included are rare insights into hundreds of gold, silver, copper and other mines in this famous Arizona mining area. Details include the locations, geology, history, production and other facts of the mines of this region. 8.5" X 11", 394 ppgs. Retail Price: $24.99

Mining in the Bisbee Quadrangle of Arizona - Originally published in 1906, this important publication on Arizona Mining has not been available for nearly a century. Included are rare insights into hundreds of gold, silver, copper and other mines in this famous Arizona mining area. Details include the locations, geology, history, production and other facts of the mines of this important mining region. 8.5" X 11", 188 ppgs. Retail Price: $14.99

Montana Mining Books

A History of Butte Montana: The World's Greatest Mining Camp - First published in 1900 by H.C. Freeman, this important publication sheds a bright light on one of the most important mining areas in the history of The West. Together with his insights, as well as rare photographs of the periods, Harry Freeman describes Butte and its vicinity from its early beginnings, right up to its flush years when copper flowed from its mines like a river. At the time of publication, Butte, Montana was known worldwide as "The Richest Mining Spot On Earth" and produced not only vast amounts of copper, but also silver, gold and other metals from its mines. Freeman illustrates, with great detail, the most important mines in the vicinity of Butte, providing rare details on their owners, their history and most importantly, how the mines operated and how their treasures were extracted. Of particular interest are the dozens of rare photographs that depict mines such as the famous Anaconda, the Silver Bow, the Smoke House, Moose, Paulin, Buffalo, Little Minah, the Mountain Consolidated, West Greyrock, Cora, the Green Mountain, Diamond, Bell, Parnell, the Neversweat, Nipper, Original and many others.   8.5" X 11", 142 ppgs. Retail Price: $12.99

The Butte Mining District of Montana - This important publication on Montana Mining has not been available for over a century. Included are rare insights into the gold, copper and silver mines of Butte, Montana together with hard to find maps and photographs. Some of the topics include the early history of gold, silver and copper mining in the Butte area, insight into the geology of its mining areas, the local distribution of gold, silver and copper ores, as well their composition and how to identify them. Also included are detailed facts about the mines in the Butte Mining District, including the famous Anaconda Mine, Gagnon, Parrot, Blue Vein, Moscow, Poulin, Stella, Buffalo, Green Mountain, Wake Up Jim, the Diamond-Bell Group, Mountain Consolidated, East Greyrock, West Greyrock, Snowball, Corra, Speculator, Adirondack, Miners Union, the Jessie-Edith May Group, Otisco, Iduna, Colorado, Lizzie, Cambers, Anderson, Hesperus, Preferencia and dozens of others. 8.5" X 11", 298 ppgs. Retail Price: $24.99

Mines of the Helena Mining Region of Montana - This important publication on Montana Mining has not been available for over a century. Included are rare insights into the gold, copper and silver mines of the vicinity of Helena, Montana, including the Marysville Mining District, Elliston Mining District, Rimini Mining District, Helena Mining District, Clancy Mining District, Wickes Mining District, Boulder and Basin Mining Districts and the Elkhorn Mining District. Some of the topics include the early history of gold, silver and copper mining in the Helena area, insight into the geology of its mining areas, the local distribution of gold, silver and copper ores, as well their composition and how to identify them. Also included are detailed facts, history, geology and locations of over one hundred gold, silver and copper mines in the area . 8.5" X 11", 162 ppgs, Retail Price: $14.99

Mines and Geology of the Garnet Range of Montana - This important publication on Montana Mining has not been available for over a century. Included are rare insights into the gold, copper and silver mines of the vicinity of this important mining area of Montana. Some of the topics include the early history of gold, silver and copper mining in the Garnet Mountains, insight into the geology of its mining areas, the local distribution of gold, silver and copper ores, as well their composition and how to identify them. Also included are detailed facts, history, geology and locations of numerous gold, silver and copper mines in the area . 8.5" X 11", 100 ppgs, Retail Price: $11.99

Mines and Geology of the Philipsburg Quadrangle of Montana - This important publication on Montana Mining has not been available for over a century. Included are rare insights into the gold, copper and silver mines of the vicinity of this important mining area of Montana. Some of the topics include the early history of gold, silver and copper mining in the Philipsburg Quadrangle, insight into the geology of its mining areas, the local distribution of gold, silver and copper ores, as well their composition and how to identify them. Also included are detailed facts, history, geology and locations of over one hundred gold, silver and copper mines in the area 8.5" X 11", 290 ppgs, Retail Price: $24.99

Geology of the Marysville Mining District of Montana - Included are rare insights into the mining geology of the Marysville Mining District. Some of the topics include the early history of gold, silver and copper mining in the area, insight into the geology of its mining areas, the local distribution of gold, silver and copper ores, as well their composition and how to identify them. Also included are detailed facts, history, geology and locations of gold, silver and copper mines in the area 8.5" X 11", 198 ppgs, Retail Price: $19.99

The Geology and Mines of Northern Idaho and North Western Montana

See listing under Idaho.

Nevada Mining Books

The Bull Frog Mining District of Nevada - Unavailable since 1910, this publication was originally compiled by the United States Department of Interior. This volume also includes important insights into the geologic formations, faults and other aspects of economic geology in this Nevada mining district. Of particular interest are the fine details on many mines in the area, including their locations, histories, development and mineralization. Some of the mines featured include the National Bank Mine, Providence, Gibraltor, Tramps, Denver, Original Bullfrog, Gold Bar, Mayflower, Homestake-King and other mines and prospects. **8.5" X 11", 152 ppgs, Retail Price: $14.99**

History of the Comstock Lode - Unavailable since 1876, this publication was originally released by John Wiley & Sons. This volume also includes important insights into the famous Comstock Lode of Nevada that represented the first major silver discovery in the United States. During its spectacular run, the Comstock produced over 192 million ounces of silver and 8.2 million ounces of gold. Not only did the Comstock result in one of the largest mining rushes in history and yield immense fortunes for its owners, but it made important contributions to the development of the State of Nevada, as well as neighboring California. Included here are important details on not only the early development and history of the Comstock, but also rare early insight into its mines, ore and its geology. **8.5" X 11", 244 ppgs, Retail Price: $19.99**

Colorado Mining Books

Ores of The Leadville Mining District - Unavailable since 1926, this publication was originally compiled by the United States Department of Interior. This volume also includes important insights into the ores and mineralization of the Leadville Mining District in Colorado. Topics include historic ore prospecting methods, local geology, insights into ore veins and stockworks, the local trend and distribution of ore channels, reverse faults, shattered rock above replacement ore bodies, mineral enrichment in oxidized and sulphide zones and more. **8.5" X 11", 66 ppgs, Retail Price: $8.99**

Mining in Colorado - Unavailable since 1926, this publication was originally compiled by the United States Department of Interior. This volume also includes important insights into the mining history of Colorado from its early beginnings in the 1850's right up to the mid 1920's. Not only is Colorado's gold mining heritage included, but also its silver, copper, lead and zinc mining industry. Each mining area is treated separately, detailing the development of Colorado's mines on a county by county basis. **8.5" X 11", 284 ppgs, Retail Price: $19.99**

Gold Mining in Gilpin County Colorado - Unavailable since 1876, this publication was originally compiled by the Register Steam Printing House of Central City, Colorado. A rare glimpse at the gold mining history and early mines of Gilpin County, Colorado from their first discovery in the 1850's up to the "flush years" of the mid 1870's. Of particular interest is the history of the discovery of gold in Gilpin County and details about the men who made those first strikes. Special focus is given to the early gold mines and first mining districts of the area, many of which are not detailed in other books on Colorado's gold mining history. **8.5" X 11", 156 ppgs, Retail Price: $12.99**

Mining in the Gold Brick Mining District of Colorado - Important insights into the history of the Gold Brick Mining District, as well as its local geography and economic geology. Also included are the histories and locations of historic mines in this important Colorado Mining District, including the Cortland, Carter, Raymond, Gold Links, Sacramento, Bassick, Sandy Hook, Chronicle, Grand Prize, Chloride, Granite Mountain, Lucille, Gray Mountain, Hilltop, Maggie Mitchell, Silver Islet, Revenue, Roosevelt, Carbonate King and others. In addition to hardrock mining, are also included are details on gold placer mining in this portion of Colorado. **8.5" X 11", 140 ppgs, Retail Price: $12.99**

Washington Mining Books

The Republic Mining District of Washington - Unavailable since 1910, this important publication was originally published by the Washington Geologic Survey and has been unavailable for a century. Topics include the geology, rock formations and the formation of ore deposits in this important mining area of Washington State. Also included are hard to find details on the geology, history and locations of dozens of mines in the area. Some of the mines featured include the New Republic Mine, Ben Hur, Morning Glory, the South Republic Mine, Quilp, Surprise, Black Tail, Lone Pine, San Poil, Mountain Lion, Tom Thumb, Elcaliph and many others. **8.5" X 11", 94 ppgs, Retail Price: $10.99**

The Myers Creek and Nighthawk Mining Districts of Washington - Unavailable since 1911, this important publication was originally published by the Washington Geologic Survey and has been unavailable for a century. Topics include the geology, rock formations and the formation of ore deposits in these important mining areas of Washington State. Also included are hard to find details on the geology, history and locations of dozens of mines in the area. Some of the mines featured include the Grant Mine, Monterey, Nip and Tuck, Myers Creek, Number Nine, Neutral, Rainbow, Aztec, Crystal Butte, Apex, Butcher Boy, Molson, Mad River, Olentangy, Delate, Kelsey, Golden Chariot, Okanogan, Ohio, Forty-Ninth Parallel, Nighthawk, Favorite, Little Chopaka, Summit, Number One, California, Peerless, Caaba, Prize Group, Ruby, Mountain Sheep, Golden Zone, Rich Bar, Similkameen, Kimberly, Triune, Hiawatha, Trinity, Hornsilver, Maquae, Bellevue, Bullfrog, Palmer Lake, Ivanhoe, Copper World and many others. **8.5" X 11", 136 ppgs, Retail Price: $12.99**

The Blewett Mining District of Washington - Unavailable since 1911, this important publication was originally published by the Washington Geologic Survey and has been unavailable for a century. Topics include the geology, rock formations and the formation of ore deposits in this important mining area of Washington State. Also included are hard to find details on the geology, history and locations of dozens of mines in the area. Some of the mines featured include the Washington Meteor, Alta Vista, Pole Pick, Blinn, North Star, Golden Eagle, Tip Top, Wilder, Golden Guinea, Lucky Queen, Blue Bell, Prospect, Homestake, Lone Rock, Johnson, and others. **8.5" X 11", 134 ppgs, Retail Price: $12.99**

Silver Mining In Washington - Unavailable since 1955, this important publication was originally published by the Washington Geologic Survey. Featured are the hard to find locations and details pertaining to Washington's silver mines. **8.5" X 11", 180 ppgs, Retail Price: $15.99**

The Mines of Snohomish County Washington - Unavailable since 1942, this important publication was originally published by the Washington Geologic Survey and has been unavailable for seventy years. Featured are details on a large number of gold, silver, copper, lead and other metallic mineral mines. Included are the locations of each historic mine, along with information on the commodity produced. **8.5" X 11", 98 ppgs, Retail Price: $10.99**

The Mines of Chelan County Washington - Unavailable since 1943, this important publication was originally published by the Washington Geologic Survey and has been unavailable for seventy years. Featured are details on a large number of gold, silver, copper, lead and other metallic mineral mines. Included are the locations of each historic mine, along with information on the commodity. **8.5" X 11", 88 ppgs, Retail Price: $9.99**

Metal Mines of Washington - Unavailable since 1921, this important publication was originally published by the Washington Geologic Survey and has been unavailable for nearly ninety years. Widely considered a masterpiece on the Washington Mining Industry, "Metal Mines of Washington" sheds light on the important details of Washington's early mining years. Featured are details on hundreds of gold, silver, copper, lead and other metallic mineral mines. Included are hard to find details on the mineral resources of this state, as well as the locations of historic mines. Lavishly illustrated with maps and historic photos and complete with a glossary to explain any technical terms found in the text, this is one of the most important works on mining in the State of Washington. No prospector or miner should be without it if they are interested in mining in Washington. **8.5" X 11", 396 ppgs, Retail Price: $24.99**

Gem Stones In Washington - Unavailable since 1949, this important publication was originally published by the Washington Geologic Survey and has been unavailable since first published. Included are details on where to find naturally occurring gem stones in the State of Washington, including quartz crystal, amethyst, smoky quartz, milky quartz, agates, bloodstone, carnelian, chert, flint, jasper, onyx, petrified wood, opal, fire opal, hyalite and others. **8.5" X 11", 54 ppgs, Retail Price: $8.99**

The Covada Mining District of Washington - Unavailable since 1913, this important publication was originally published by the Washington Geologic Survey and has been unavailable for a century. Topics include the geology, rock formations and the formation of ore deposits in this important mining area of Washington State. Also included are hard to find details on the geology, history and locations of dozens of mines in the area. Some of the mines featured include the Admiral, Advance, Algonkian, Big Bug, Big Chief, Big Joker, Black Hawk, Black Tail, Black Thorn, Captain, Cherokee Strip, Colorado, Dan Patch, Dead Shot, Etta, Good Ore, Greasy Run, Great Scott, Idora, IXL, Jay Bird, Kentucky Bell, King Solomon, Laurel, Laura S, Little Jay, Meteor, Neglected, Northern Light, Old Nell, Plymouth Rock, Polaris, Quandary, Reserve, Shoo Fly, Silver Plume, Three Pines, Vernie, White Rose and dozens of others. **8.5" X 11", 114 ppgs, Retail Price: $10.99**

The Index Mining District of Washington - Unavailable since 1912, this important publication was originally published by the Washington Geologic Survey and has been unavailable for a century. Topics include the geology, rock formations and the formation of ore deposits in this important mining area of Washington State. Also included are hard to find details on the geology, history and locations of dozens of mines in the area. Some of the mines featured include the Sunset, Non-Pareil, Ethel Consolidated, Kittaning, Merchant, Homestead, Co-operative, Lost Creek, Uncle Sam, Calumet, Florence-Rae, Bitter Creek, Index Peacock, Gunn Peak, Helena, North Star, Buckeye. Copper Bell, Red Cross and others. **8.5" X 11", 114 ppgs, Retail Price: $11.99**

Mining & Mineral Resources of Stevens County Washington – Unavailable since 1920, this important publication was originally published by the Washington Geologic Survey and has been unavailable for a century. Topics include the geology, rock formations and the formation of ore deposits in these important mining areas of Washington State. Also included are hard to find details on the geology, history and locations of hundreds of mines in the area. **8.5" X 11", 372 ppgs, Retail Price: $24.99**

The Mines and Geology of the Loomis Quadrangle Okanogan County, Washington – Unavailable since 1972, this important publication was originally published by the Washington Geologic Survey and has been unavailable for a century. Topics include the geology, rock formations and the formation of ore deposits in this important mining area of Washington State. Also included are hard to find details on the geology, history and locations of dozens of gold, copper, silver and other mines in the area. **8.5" X 11", 150 ppgs, Retail Price: $12.99**

The Conconully Mining District of Okanogan County Washington – Unavailable since 1973, this important publication was originally published by the Washington Geologic Survey and has been unavailable for a century. Topics include the geology, rock formations and the formation of ore deposits in this important mining area of Washington State, which also includes Salmon Creek, Blue Lake and Galena. Also included are hard to find details on the geology, mining history and locations of dozens of mines in the area. Some of the mines include Arlington, Fourth of July, Sonny Boy, First Thought, Last Chance, War Eagle-Peacock, Wheeler, Mohawk, Lone Star, Woo Loo Moo Loo, Keystone, Hughes, Plant-Callahan, Johnny Boy, Leuena, Gubser, John Arthur, Tough Nut, Homestake, Key and many others **8.5" X 11", 68 ppgs, Retail Price: $8.99**

Wyoming Mining Books

Mining in the Laramie Basin of Wyoming – Unavailable since 1909, this publication was originally compiled by the United States Department of Interior. Also included are insights into the mineralization and other characteristics of this important mining region, especially in regards to coal, limestone, gypsum, bentonite clay, cement, sand, clay and copper. **8.5" X 11", 104 ppgs, Retail Price: $11.99**

New Mexico Mining Books

The Mogollon Mining District of New Mexico – Unavailable since 1927, this important publication was originally published by the US Department of Interior and has been unavailable for 80 years. Topics include the geology, rock formations and the formation of ore deposits in this important mining area in New Mexico. Of particular focus is information on the history and production of the ore deposits in this area, their form and structure, vein filling, their paragenesis, origins and ore shoots, as well as oxidation and supergene enrichment. Also included are hard to find details, including the descriptions and locations of numerous gold, silver and other types of mines, including the Eureka, Pacific, South Alpine, Great Western, Enterprise, Buffalo, Mountain View, Floride, Gold Dust, Last Chance, Deadwood, Confidence, Maud S., Deep Down, Little Fanney, Trilby, Johnson, Alberta, Comet, Golden Eagle, Cooney, Queen, the Iron Crown, Eberle, Clifton, Andrew Jackson mine, Mascot and others. **8.5" X 11", 144 ppgs, Retail Price: $12.99**

The Percha Mining District of Kingston New Mexico – Unavailable since 1883, this important publication was originally published by the Kingston Tribune and has been unavailable for over one hundred and thirty five years. Having been written during the earliest years of gold and silver mining in the Percha Mining District, unlike other books on the subject, this work offers the unique perspective of having actually been written while the early mining history of this area was still being made. In fact, the work was written so early in the development of this area that many of the notable mines in the Percha District were less than a few years old and were still being operated by their original discoverers with the same enthusiasm as when they were first located. Included are hard to find details on the very earliest gold and silver mines of this important mining district near Kingston in Sierra County, New Mexico. **8.5" X 11", 68 ppgs, Retail Price: $9.99**

East Coast Mining Books

The Gold Fields of the Southern Appalachians – Unavailable since 1895, this important publication was originally published by the US Department of Interior and has been unavailable for nearly 120 years. Topics include the geology, rock formations and the formation of ore deposits in this important mining area of the American South. Of particular focus is information on the history and statistics of the ore deposits in this area, their form and structure and veins. Also included are details on the placer gold deposits of the region. The gold fields of the Georgian Belt, Carolinian Belt and the South Mountain Mining District of North Carolina are all treated in descriptive detail. Included are hard to find details, including the descriptions and locations of numerous gold mines in Georgia, North Carolina and elsewhere in the American South. Also included are details on the gold belts of the British Maritime Provinces and the Green Mountains. **8.5" X 11", 104 ppgs, Retail Price: $9.99**

Gold Rush Tales Series

Millions in Siskiyou County Gold - In this first volume of the "Gold Rush Tales" series, leading mining historian and editor Kerby Jackson, introduces us to the story of how millions of dollars worth of gold was discovered in Siskiyou County during the California Gold Rush. Lavishly illustrated with photos from the 19th Century, this hard to find information was first published in 1897 and sheds important light onto the gold rush era in Siskiyou County, California and the experiences of the men who dug for the gold and actually found it. **8.5" X 11", 82 ppgs, Retail Price: $9.99**

The California Rand in the Days of '49 - In this second volume of the "Gold Rush Tales" series, leading mining historian and editor Kerby Jackson, introduces us to four tales from the California Gold Rush. Lavishly illustrated with photos from the 19th Century, this hard to find information was first published in 1890's and includes the stories of "California's Rand", details about Chinese miners, how one early miner named Baker struck it rich and also the story of Alphonzo Bowers, who invented the first hydraulic gold dredge. **8.5" X 11", 54 ppgs, Retail Price: $9.99**

More Mining Books

Prospecting and Developing A Small Mine - Topics covered include the classification of varying ores, how to take a proper ore sample, the proper reduction of ore samples, alluvial sampling, how to understand geology as it is applied to prospecting and mining, prospecting procedures, methods of ore treatment, the application of drilling and blasting in a small mine and other topics that the small scale miner will find of benefit. **8.5" X 11", 112 ppgs, Retail Price: $11.99**

Timbering For Small Underground Mines - Topics covered include the selection of caps and posts, the treatment of mine timbers, how to install mine timbers, repairing damaged timbers, use of drift supports, headboards, squeeze sets, ore chute construction, mine cribbing, square set timbering methods, the use of steel and concrete sets and other topics that the small underground miner will find of benefit. This volume also includes twenty eight illustrations depicting the proper construction of mine timbering and support systems that greatly enhance the practical usability of the information contained in this small book. **8.5" X 11", 88 ppgs. Retail Price: $10.99**

Timbering and Mining - A classic mining publication on Hard Rock Mining by W.H. Storms. Unavailable since 1909, this rare publication provides an in depth look at American methods of underground mine timbering and mining methods. Topics include the selection and preservation of mine timbers, drifting and drift sets, driving in running ground, structural steel in mine workings, timbering drifts in gravel mines, timbering methods for driving shafts, positioning drill holes in shafts, timbering stations at shafts, drainage, mining large ore bodies by means of open cuts or by the "Glory Hole" system, stoping out ore in flat or low lying veins, use of the "Caving System", stoping in swelling ground, how to stope out large ore bodies, Square Set timbering on the Comstock and its modifications by California miners, the construction of ore chutes, stoping ore bodies by use of the "Block System", how to work dangerous ground, information on the "Delprat System" of stoping without mine timbers, construction and use of headframes and much more. This volume provides a reference into not only practical methods of mining and timbering that may be employed in narrow vein mining by small miners today, but also rare insights into how mines were being worked at the turn of the 19th Century. **8.5" X 11", 288 ppgs. Retail Price: $24.99**

A Study of Ore Deposits For The Practical Miner - Mining historian Kerby Jackson introduces us to a classic mining publication on ore deposits by J.P. Wallace. First published in 1908, it has been unavailable for over a century. Included are important insights into the properties of minerals and their identification, on the occurrence and origin of gold, on gold alloys, insights into gold bearing sulfides such as pyrites and arsenopyrites, on gold bearing vanadium, gold and silver tellurides, lead and mercury tellurides, on silver ores, platinum and iridium, mercury ores, copper ores, lead ores, zinc ores, iron ores, chromium ores, manganese ores, nickel ores, tin ores, tungsten ores and others. Also included are facts regarding rock forming minerals, their composition and occurrences, on igneous, sedimentary, metamorphic and intrusive rocks, as well as how they are geologically disturbed by dikes, flows and faults, as well as the effects of these geologic actions and why they are important to the miner. Written specifically with the common miner and prospector in mind, the book will help to unlock the earth's hidden wealth for you and is written in a simple and concise language that anyone can understand. **8.5" X 11", 366 ppgs. Retail Price: $24.99**

Mine Drainage - Unavailable since 1896, this rare publication provides an in depth look at American methods of underground mine drainage and mining pump systems. This volume provides a reference into not only practical methods of mining drainage that may be employed in narrow vein mining by small miners today, but also rare insights into how mines were being worked at the turn of the 19th Century. **8.5" X 11", 218 ppgs. Retail Price: $24.99**

Fire Assaying Gold, Silver and Lead Ores - Unavailable since 1907, this important publication was originally published by the Mining and Scientific Press and was designed to introduce miners and prospectors of gold, silver and lead to the art of fire assaying. Topics include the fire assaying of ores and products containing gold, silver and lead; the sampling and preparation of ore for an assay; care of the assay office, assay furnaces; crucibles and scorifiers; assay balances; metallic ores; scorification assays; cupelling; parting' crucible assays, the roasting of ores and more. This classic provides a time honored method of assaying put forward in a clear, concise and easy to understand language that will make it a benefit to even beginners. **8.5" X 11", 96 ppgs. Retail Price: $11.99**

Methods of Mine Timbering - Originally published in 1896, this important publication on mining engineering has not been available for nearly a century. Included are rare insights into historical methods of timbering structural support that were used in underground metal mines during the California that still have a practical application for the small scale hardrock miner of today. **8.5" X 11", 94 ppgs. Retail Price: $10.99**

The Enrichment of Copper Sulfide Ores - First published in 1913, it has been unavailable for over a century. Topics include the definition and types of ore enrichment, the oxidation of copper ores, the precipitation of metallic sulfides. Also included are the results of dozens of lab experiments pertaining to the enrichment of sulfide ores that will be of interest to the practical hard rock mine operator in his efforts to release the metallic bounty from his mine's ore. **8.5" X 11", 92 ppgs. Retail Price: $9.99**

A Study of Magmatic Sulfide Ores - Unavailable since 1914, this rare publication provides an in depth look at magmatic sulfide ores. Some of the topics included are the definition and classification of magmatic ores, descriptions of some magmatic sulfide ore deposits known at the time of publication including copper and nickel bearing pyrrohitic ore bodies, chalcopyrite-bornite deposits, pyritic deposits, magnetite-ileminite deposits, chromite deposits and magmatic iron ore deposits. Also included are details on how to recognize these types of ore deposits while prospecting for valuable hardrock minerals. **8.5" X 11", 138 ppgs. Retail Price: $11.99**

The Cyanide Process of Gold Recovery - Unavailable since 1894 and released under the name "The Cyanide Process: Its Practical Application and Economical Results", this rare publication provides an in depth look at the early use of cyanide leaching for gold recovery from hardrock mine ores. This volume provides a reference into the early development and use of cyanide leaching to recover gold. **8.5" X 11", 162 ppgs. Retail Price: $14.99**

California Gold Milling Practices - Unavailable since 1895 and released under the name "California Gold Practices", this rare publication provides an in depth look at early methods of milling used to reduce gold ores in California during the late 19th century. This volume provides a reference into the early development and use of milling equipment during the earliest years of the California Gold Rush up to the age of the Industrial Revolution. Much of the information still applies today and will be of use to small scale miners engaging in hardrock mining. **8.5" X 11", 104 ppgs. Retail Price: $10.99**

Leaching Gold and Silver Ores With The Plattner and Kiss Processes - Mining historian Kerby Jackson introduces us to a classic mining publication on the evaluation and examination of mines and prospects by C.H. Aaron. First published in 1881, it has been unavailable for over a century and sheds important light on the leaching of gold and silver ores with the Plattner and Kiss processes. **8.5" X 11", 204 ppgs. Retail Price: $15.99**

The Metallurgy of Lead and the Desilverization of Base Bullion - First published in 1896, it has been unavailable for over a century and sheds important light on the the recovery of silver from lead based ores. Some of the topics include the properties of lead and some of its compounds, lead ores such as galenite, anglesite, cerussite and others, the distribution of lead ores throughout the United States and the sampling and assaying of lead ores. Also covered is the metallurgical treatment of lead ores, as well as the desilverization of lead by the Pattinson Process and the Parkes Process. Hofman's text has long been considered one of the most important early works on the recovery of silver from lead based ores. **8.5" X 11", 452 ppgs. Retail Price: $29.99**

Ore Sampling For Small Scale Miners - First published in 1916, it has been unavailable for over a century and sheds important light on historic methods of ore sampling in hardrock mines. Topics include how to take correct ore samples and the conditions that affect sampling, such as their subdivision and uniformity. Particular detail is given to methods of hand sampling ore bodies by grab sample, pipe sample and coning, as well as sampling by mechanical methods. Also given are insights into the screening, drying and grinding processes to achieve the most consistent sample results and much more. **8.5" X 11", 124 ppgs. Retail Price: $12.99**

The Extraction of Silver, Copper and Tin from Ores - First published in 1896, it has been unavailable for over a century and sheds important light on how historic miners recovered silver, copper and tin from their mining operations. The book is split into three sections, including a discussion on the Lixiviation of Silver Ores, the mining and treatment of copper ores as practiced at Tharsis, Spain and the smelting of tin as it was practiced by metallurgists at Pulo Brani, Singapore. Also included is an overview and analysis of these historic metal recovery methods that will be of benefit to those interested in the extraction of silver, copper and tin from small mines. **8.5" X 11", 118 ppgs. Retail Price: $14.99**

The Roasting of Gold and Silver Ores - First published in 1880, it has been unavailable for over a century and sheds important light on how historic miners recovered gold and silver rom their mining operations. Topics include details on the most important silver and free milling gold ores, methods of desulphurization of ores, methods of deoxidation, the chlorination of ores, methods and details on roasting gold and silver ores, notes on furnaces and more. Also included are details on numerous methods of gold and silver recovery, including the Ottokar Hofman's Process, the Patera Process, Kiss Process, Augustin Process, Ziervogel Process and others. **8.5" X 11", 178 ppgs. Retail Price: $19.99**

The Examination of Mines and Prospects - First published in 1912, it has been unavailable for over a century and sheds important light on how to examine and evaluate hardrock mines, prospects and lode mining claims. Sections include Mining Examinations, Structural Geology, Structural Features of Ore Deposits, Primary Ores and their Distribution, Types of Primary Ore Deposits, Primary Ore Shoots, The Primary Alteration of Wall Rocks, Alterations by Surface Agencies, Residual Ores and their Distribution, Secondary Ores and Ore Shoots and Vein Outcrops. This hard to find information is a must for those who are interested in owning a mine or who already own a lode mining claim and wish to succeed at quartz mining. **8.5" X 11", 250 ppgs. Retail Price: $19.99**

Made in the USA
San Bernardino, CA
28 February 2019